KIDS SPEAK

◇ 3 ◇

KIDS SPEAK
◇ 3 ◇

Children Talk
About Themselves

by Chaim Walder

translated by Aviva Rappaport

Illustrated by Yoni Gerstein

FELDHEIM
Jerusalem ▢ New York

Originally published in 1997 in Hebrew
as *Yeladim Mesaprim al Atzmam* (Vol. 3)

First published 1997
ISBN 0-87306-830-0

FELDHEIM PUBLISHERS
POB 35002 / Jerusalem Israel

200 Airport Executive Park
Nanuet, NY 10954

10 9 8 7 6 5 4 3 2

typeset at Rappaport, Jerusalem

Printed in Israel

Approbation for Volume One from **Rabbi Yitzchak Silberstein**, *shlita*

הנושא של חינוך הילדים, לתורה, ויר"ש ומדות טובות, תופס מקום בראש, של כל יהודי, ומלאכת החינוך דורשת עיון. מחשבה ותושיה, ועל כולם תפילה בכל לב להשי"ת. הרב חיים ולדר שליט"א בתור מחנך, בא לעזור להורים בעצה וחכמה כיצד לעזור לילדיהם להתגבר על בעיות המפריעות להם. הבה ונחזיק לו טובה על כך.

דכירנא, בלומדנו בישיבת סלבודקה, בא תלמיד לפני ראש הישיבה הגה"צ ר' אייזיק שר זצ"ל וסיפר לו על חברו בחדר האוכל שמשוחח כל היום על רכישת מעלות חמריות, וממון, ושאל את ראש הישיבה כיצד להתגבר על כך, שלא יושפע מחבירו? וגם ביקש להרחיק את החבר משכנותו!

כנראה שראש הישיבה זצ"ל ראה בדברי בחור זה, קצת יהירות, אמר לו: החובת לבבות מודה להשי"ת על כל טובותיו, שגמל עמו ואחד מהם היא שמחשבותיו נסתרות ואין איש יודע ומכירם, אחרת היו חבריו בורחים ממנו..., אם היו יודעים מחשבותיו! אם אתה גם היית חושב כך, היית דואג על נגעי לבבך, ולא היית שם לב לנגעי חברך.

והשי"ת יעזרנו ללמוד וללמד לעשות הישר בעיניו   **יצחק זילברשטיין**

Approbation for Volume One from **Rabbi Avraham Gombo**, *shlita*

להר"ר חיים ולדר שיחי'

ראיתי את ספרך היפה והחינוכי והיתה לי זו שעה של קורת רוח ושמחה ואכן ראויים הדברים למי שכותבם.

שהרי העיקר בעובדתינו החינוכית היא הקניית הרגלי חשיבה נכונים ומידות טובות לתלמידים ובפרט בהנהגות שבין תלמיד לרעהו.

ואישיות כמוך המכיר את נפש הילד והנמצא עמהם בבעיותיהם התמידיות יודע יפה כיצד להביע בכתב את קשייהם לבטיהם ופתרונותיהם כאחד בבעיות היום יום של ה"בין אדם לחבירו".

יה"ר וחפץ ד' בידך יצליח, ודפי הספר יפיקו את התועלת הנכספת, והיא לבנות תלמידים צעירי הצאן הבנים במידות טובות ובדרך ארץ שהם מקניני התורה הקדושה.

בברכה והערכה   **אברהם ישראל גומבו**

תלמוד תורה
דקהלת
"משכנות יעקב"

רחי אורי חיים 28
בני-ברק
טל. 03-6743328

בס"ד

תאריך צאן לסדר אחד עולם עונג ישעהו
(ולא ימוש הגבורה) תשנ"ב

לכידי הרב חיים ולדר שליט"א

בכפלתי עברתי על רוב גבי הספרים בסברק לידיי שמהדים על עניני
הלך שני וכבוד שלד. כי שיוי אפיים אותק הפונדתק בנער הולוק לשנק
יורד על הילד ומי אות גביעטו וחולק אל פעילו בכתיבו שי ובכן אלהם אתגיו,
ובצבית חלק שני דרק הספר של הלידם. שהי יוצא ידיה שלמית
בכצירת ולבצמית אין לריב ול אינם ברקיים שו להם של או לבן ול להבטיר
אין הריציה. ובעת לפנני ספר הבצג בתיגית לנדלות הלקחים אעולה
דמיון לי הילד או לומד לקח מן האבאות נילוחת אות, ונברה עדת
להתגירם שלד וי נעצגה לפתחין לדניה ודמינים. והבלוה.
ספרי קריא היני בטרה שנה ועי ידי גב עם נעלה אעלא.

ושימעו לצלכם חבל, שר.

בידיית וגהדצרם
יצתן בריך

Approbation for Volume Two from **Rabbi Yitzchak Fried**, shlita

*To the dear members of my family in the
United States*

*Yaakov and Tova Mendelowitz
& Family*

and

*Avraham Yosef and Pesia Frankel
& Family*

To My Young Readers

Three years have passed since MORE KIDS SPEAK was published. During the interim, I have *b'ezras Hashem* published a book for adults, LISTEN TO THE SOUL! and a book for young adults, THAT'S ME, TZVIKI GREEN!

Three years is too long a time, and many people wondered why I was in no hurry to publish a third volume of KIDS SPEAK.

The answer is that I wanted to remain faithful to the original idea behind the book — the desire to give expression to the world of children, their thoughts, struggles, joys and sorrows. For there is no lack of stories in our world — take a road, a car, and an accident, and you have a story. But a moving story that touches the heart, a story that lets a reader identify with its characters and makes him feel that it is talking about him and helping him — stories like these are rarer.

That is why I did not rush, but instead waited patiently for the right stories to come my way and gather together into an interesting, helpful book. For this is what I once promised myself — to make my books interesting and helpful.

The stories presented here portray the world of twenty-three children, the situations they encountered, and the ways they dealt with them. I hope you will find in this book, as you did in my previous books, figures with whom you can identify.

If you haven't yet written to KIDS SPEAK, POB 211, BNEI BRAK, ISRAEL, like the many thousands of children in Israel and all over the world who have, now is the time to do so. Maybe you will find yourself — with a fictitious name and details changed — in the next book!

Chaim Walder

Contents

The Cave Man

My name is Eli. I live in Haifa and I'm in the seventh grade.

I'm an ordinary kid, not too quiet and not too loud. I'm a little short, a little skinny, and I have blue eyes.

Every Shabbos afternoon, ever since I was in the third grade, I've always gone to shul to study a little with my friends. After that, we go for a walk and talk.

Usually, we go to Maonot Geula, a beautiful neighborhood that's just above the Vizhnitz housing complex. Right in the middle there's a nice park that has a path leading from it to the houses.

We first discovered the cave when I was in the fourth grade. At the edge of the park there's a path that's not paved. It leads right into a huge cave. We used to stand at the end of the path and try to peek into the cave.

One Shabbos, Tzviki, one of my friends, suggested that we go off the path to see the cave from the inside. We walked into the cave fearfully. Right inside the entrance we found a lot of cartons, all arranged in perfect order. There were also hundreds of old car tires stacked on each other blocking the opening to the cave, plus a small wooden gate. We decided that some kids must have built it all. We were curious to see the cave from the inside.

We went further in.

I never saw anything like it in my life. Someone had spent a lot of time working inside the cave. Whoever it was had built walls out of tires, plastic containers and cartons. Other pieces of junk, too many to count, were also stacked up in amazing order.

There was a huge pile of plates, there were old forks and spoons all arranged perfectly, and endless piles of clothes. It was simply amazing, fascinating, and slightly scary.

We walked in astonishment between the orderly piles, and then Shaiki said, "Who knows — maybe this is a robber's cave!"

Suddenly, we were scared stiff.

"Let's go," I said.

"What for? There's no one here," said Tzviki, who lived in Vizhnitz.

We continued to roam around.

Suddenly I spotted an inner recess that was partly hidden by a dirty curtain.

"I wonder what's behind this curtain," I said, pulling it aside fast...

"Immaaaa!" I screamed. "Immaaaa!"

There was a man behind the curtain. He was lying on a mattress of cartons. When he saw me, he shouted a scary "BOO!" and jumped out of the bed. There was only one step between us. He almost caught me, but the shock woke me up and I started to run away.

We made our way through the stacks of cartons. I'll never forget how frightened I was. It was the scariest thing that ever happened to me in my whole life.

We ran out of the cave to safety as fast as our legs could carry us. Only after we made it to the park, to where some fathers were watching their children, did we feel safe.

He came out after us and stood at the edge of the park. He was dressed in rags, his pants tied with a rope instead of a belt. He was wearing two boots that didn't match, and on his nose was the strangest pair of glasses I've ever seen, with frames made of twisted wires. He looked like he was from another planet.

The man shook his fist threateningly, then shouted a few things we couldn't understand, and disappeared way back into the cave.

I stood rooted to the spot. Pale and shaking, I felt like I had just been saved from death. Really.

I looked at Shaiki. He was also trembling, and covered with cold sweat. Only Tzviki was calm and relaxed.

"What's the matter? Don't you know who that is?" he said. "That's the Cave Man!"

"You know him?" I asked.

"Sure," said Tzviki. "He's been living here since I was born and even before that. My big brother even played chess with him."

"He knows what chess is?" I asked.

"He's a master player," said Tzviki. "He has a chess board made of cardboard that he made himself, and pieces that he carved from wood."

For a while, Tzviki sat and told us what he knew about the Cave Man. The sun was about to set, so we rushed to shul for Mincha.

The next Shabbos I went to the park along with another five of my friends, planning on going into the cave again. I was still afraid of the Cave Man, but at least I knew what to watch out for.

This is where the part I'm a little ashamed to tell you starts. Still, I made up my mind to tell.

When we got to the cave, we were pretty scared about going inside. We looked down from above and tried to see the Cave Man. It didn't work.

Someone started to shout, "Cave Man, come out!" After that, we all started to shout the same thing.

The shouts turned into taunts. I can't explain why we did it. We were just little kids. We didn't think about it too much.

When our taunts weren't answered, one of us started to throw heavy chunks of dirt towards the cave. They smashed the piles of cartons and made a big noise.

Suddenly, he darted out of the cave.

"Imma'le!" we screamed and fled in all directions.

He ran after us as fast as lightening, even though he was very old. It was really scary to see that man dressed in tatters, running and making strange sounds. We could only make out one word "Bombs," and then another word that he kept repeating: "Germans." We didn't understand the shouts, and that was even more frightening. He kept on running, until he gave up and went back slowly to the cave.

At first, we were breathless and shaking with fright. Then, after a few minutes, we started going back closer to the cave. Again, the same thing happened. We yelled into the cave, threw clods of dirt, he came running out again, shouting "Bombs!" and we scattered in fear.

We were acting mean. Plain and simple.

The following Shabbos and the ones after it, we came with reinforcements. We acted like a bunch of wild kids. We kept on tormenting the strange man in the cave, and he, for his part, came out every once in a while to chase after us. To us, it seemed like a game — a dangerous game, but still a game.

Although we went there only on Shabbos, we'd talk about what happened throughout the entire week. We imagined ourselves to be in the middle of a war against the dangerous man in the cave, a war that we were, of course, winning. I remember that I used to dream at night about how he'd chase me and I'd run away. And, as you all know, in dreams it's very hard to run away, because you always feel that you're running but staying in the same place and that your enemy is catching up to you.

We didn't look at it as tormenting a helpless old man. Maybe because he didn't look so helpless. With his strange clothes and his knife tucked into a special sheath, he didn't look helpless at all.

Then, one day, I think it was a Monday, Tzviki came to school very excited.

"Yesterday they brought a giant tractor to the cave. They started to close up the Cave

Man's cave with dirt. You won't believe what happened — he didn't want to come out! He shouted and acted crazy. A few workers went into the cave and started to look for him. They didn't find him. He had disappeared deep inside. They called the police and a few policemen went inside to look — but they didn't find him, either.

"They decided to stop work on closing up the cave because they were afraid the Cave Man might be trapped inside. I was next to the policemen and I heard them say that today they were going to find him and take him out by force and then close up the cave forever."

Tzviki talked and talked and we bombarded him with questions. If you'd have asked me, well, I wasn't that happy about it, not at all. We decided to go to the cave right after school.

When we got there, we saw something very strange. A lot of people, including some police-men, went in and out of the cave carrying cartons, rags, and hundreds of tires. They piled the "merchandise" on trucks, which drove off to dump the junk and then returned. The workers kept complaining about the work forced on them. One of them said to us, "The plan was to close up the opening of the cave without taking out the junk. That would have been quick and easy. But that wise guy is hiding inside and until they find him, we can't begin to seal it."

With my own eyes I saw how truck after truck was filled and carted away, yet the cave was still full of things that the Cave Man had collected over many years.

But the Cave Man himself still hadn't been found.

Tractors began to go into the cave. It seemed that the municipal workers who were brought to the place just weren't willing to give up on emptying the cave. As the work progressed, new mountains of junk had been discovered, so they decided to bring the tractors into the cave.

We watched open-eyed at everything that was going on. The tractors made a huge amount of noise. One of them hit the roof of the cave with its shovel and giant rocks chipped off. That's when we heard the shouts. They were blood curdling. Some of them were in Yiddish, some of them were in Hebrew. "Save me!" "They're coming to bomb me!" "Mama, Tatte!"

Everyone looked to see where the voice was coming from, but the way the cave was built made it hard to find the source of the sound, which sounded like a thousand echoes repeating themselves.

Suddenly one of the policemen shouted, "There he is!"

The Cave Man was seen racing out of the cave. He ran as we had never seen him run before. He escaped to the hill above the cave. A few policemen started to chase after him, but in the end, they returned the same way they had come.

The police captain didn't seem worried. Not at all. "There's no need for us to catch him," he said. "Now we can close up the cave without going to the trouble of taking out the junk."

The tractors came out of the cave and began to push tons of sand and dirt back into it. Within an hour and a half they had completely sealed it. What had once been a cave with paths, "streets," and rooms, had turned into a flat plain of sand, with only the roof of the cave poking down here and there.

Suddenly Tzviki's father appeared. He looked sad. Very sad.

"How could they do something like this?" we heard him murmur. "How could they?"

We looked at him and didn't understand what he meant.

"Abba, do you know him?" asked Tzviki.

"And how. Twenty years ago, before he went crazy, he sat in shul right in front of me," said Tzviki's father.

This was really surprising.

"Do you mean to say that once—"

"Come, and I'll tell you the story," said Tzviki's father.

"His name is Meir Widelmir. He was born in Warsaw in Poland. He was sixteen when the Holocaust began. Meir hid in a dark cellar in the Warsaw ghetto.

"For a year he managed to make short trips outside to get food, until the uprising broke out in the ghetto — the uprising that he took part in. The Jewish revolt succeeded at first, but was soon put down by the Germans. They bombed the ghetto, destroying it completely.

"Through a miracle, Meir survived in the ruins. He remained alive, and after the war he made aliyah to *Eretz Yisrael*. Yet, apparently, the difficult events he went through left their mark on his soul. He arrived in Haifa. He never married. He worked at all kinds of odd jobs before the breakdown.

"The breakdown happened twenty years ago, during the Yom Kippur war. During one of the air raids, when everyone ran down to the shelters, Meir was seen running through the streets, pointing to the sky and shouting, 'Bombs! Save us — the Germans are coming!'

"He disappeared from his home. They searched for him for days without finding him.

One day, someone said that they had seen him around here, on the hill. The police were called and found him sleeping on a mattress in this cave. They took him to the hospital, and there they found out that he was healthy physically, but emotionally ill. They tried to find a suitable place for him, but time after time he would suffer a terrible attack and run away crying, 'Germans! Bombs!" and all that.'

Tzviki's father stopped his story and we didn't dare look him in the face. Suddenly we understood the shouts he made when we threw chunks of earth into the cave. The tremendous noise reminded him of the Germans. Boy, were we ashamed.

I wondered if Tzviki's father knew about the terrible way we had acted. From the way he talked, I guessed not.

"I heard that recently, even here, he was tormented," said Tzviki's father. "Someone told me that children were teasing him. I don't understand what would make kids act so cruelly," he said.

We didn't say a word. Not a single one of us dared open his mouth. Tzviki was the only one to say defensively, "I'm positive that if they'd have known his story, they would never even have thought about doing something like that."

Tzviki's father didn't accept that excuse.

"And what if he was just a simple unfortunate person? Would it be okay to bother him then? What kind of an excuse is it to say, 'They didn't know'? They didn't know that it's wrong to torment a poor old man?"

Tzviki's father sighed and then stood up. Now it was too late. Who knew what would happen to the Cave Man. That cave had been a safe, cozy home for him. Now he had no place to go. What would happen to him?

Tzviki's father left.

"You started it," Yossi said to Shloimi.

"Me? Who was the first one to shout 'Cave Man'?"

"Me — but you started to throw things."

"And that makes you right? If I'd jump off the twentieth floor of a building would you follow?

"What's the connection?"

They started to fight, but I was still caught up in the Cave Man's story. All of a sudden I heard myself say, "Stop it!"

They stopped arguing and looked at me.

"Do you mind stopping now?" I said.

And I walked away.

A day passed. A week. We went a few more times to the cave to see if anything had changed, but the place looked forlorn and ne-glected. Suddenly we realized that the Cave

Man had breathed life into a deserted place and that now, after he had gone and the cave was sealed up, it was just boring.

Another two weeks passed, and one day Uzi came into class all excited. "I saw the Cave Man on Arlosoroff Street," he said.

We surrounded him and he told us the story. He had been walking down Arlosoroff next to Nordau Street when he spotted the Cave Man in Benjamin Park. Although he saw him from a distance, he was sure it was him. He was dressed in the same rags and was wearing the same glasses made of twisted wires.

After school we went to Benjamin Park.

The Cave Man was not there.

A couple of days later, Eli told us that the Cave Man had passed within a yard of him. Where? On Hermon Street at the corner of Beitar (right next to our school, which was on Ben Baba Street). Eli said that the Cave Man looked hungry, and that Yosef the falafel man had given him a few falafels.

Two days later, we saw him — me and Uzi.

He was sleeping on a bench in Struk Park, between the swings. We looked at him from across the park and really pitied him.

From that same day on, we used to see him around Struk Park. We realized that he must have decided to live in the park.

"I wonder what he does when it rains," said Uzi.

"Yeah," I said. "Until now he had a cave, and now—"

"I have an idea," said Uzi. "Let's bring him all kinds of cartons to cover himself with."

I had an even better idea. "Let's build him a little sukkah out of boards."

"Sure," said Uzi, "just try getting near him. After all, he knows what we look like."

"So what should we do?" I asked.

"We'll bring him boards, tires, and cartons, and he'll build it by himself. Believe me, he knows how to build a little bit better than you do," Uzi teased me.

Right then I wanted to answer Uzi back. I hardly ever let him get away with teasing me, but I had to admit that this time he was pretty much on target.

From that day on we started to drag over materials for building the Cave Man's new home. When he was in the park, we would put them down in a special corner, and when we'd come and he wasn't there, we would bring the boards, cartons and tires straight to the bench he slept on.

For the first few days, he didn't even touch them. We almost gave up. But then one day, when we were coming home from school, Uzi whispered to me, "Look!"

Several boards and cartons were tied to the bench that the Cave Man used to sleep on. He had piled tires on the other side of the boards so that they would stand up straight.

"He's starting to build his new house," I whispered to Uzi, and just then he appeared and we had to get out of there fast.

The "building materials" continued to pile up. That corner of Struk Park turned into a huge pile, like the piles of wood kids build before Lag Ba-Omer. The Cave Man built very slowly, at his own pace.

The "house" was up after a week. It was strong and sturdy. We saw from a distance how logically and cleverly the Cave Man built his new cave.

Still, he wasn't satisfied. He kept thickening the walls of his house. One day, we saw him add another "room." In short, the "cave" had moved from Maonot Geula to Struk Park.

But the troubles had moved along with it.

One day, we spotted a few city officials who came to the place. Resolutely they went closer to the hodge-podge building and tried to talk with the Cave Man. He refused to talk with them. They moved away and began to talk among themselves. They didn't notice that we were listening intently to their conversation. They probably thought we were just little kids. As a matter of fact, that's exactly what we were.

They talked openly about how to demolish the structure, and what to do with the illegal resident. We realized that the sad scene of the tractors that destroyed the Cave Man's home was going to repeat itself.

We talked about it amongst ourselves. Tzviki suggested that we try to stop the tractors. He had all kinds of ideas, and we were excited about them at first, but then we realized that they were just dreams. We were no match for the big men with the tractors.

Then one day, on our way home from school, I saw them. They were officials, without tractors. They had brought a few workers who were now taking apart the outer room. The Cave Man paced back and forth from side to side like a caged lion. It was obvious that he was full of sorrow.

"What are we going to do, Uzi?" I whispered.

Uzi didn't say a word; the same went for Moshe and Tzviki. After all, what could we do?

"I'm calling my father," said Tzviki. "I have an idea."

Tzviki's idea was to call up Mr. Avraham Shimmel, the only religious member of Haifa's City Council. "My father knows him. He's the only one who can help."

We ran to a pay phone. Tzviki talked fast. He told his father what was going on and his father ended the conversation by saying, "I'll call Mr. Shimmel."

We waited there. The workers had already taken down one wall. We didn't dare say anything to them. "By the time Mr. Shimmel comes, they'll already have taken down everything," I pointed out bitterly.

"I did whatever I could," apologized Tzviki.

Another wall went down. Right in front of our eyes we saw all the tires he had arranged in the second room as well as the walls of the main room of the new cave.

They took apart the whole second room and then they went on to the main one.

That room was really built well. It was hard for them to pull out the tires, the boards and the dozens of cartons which made up the wall. We recognized the cartons. We could have told you where we found each and every one.

Somehow, it seemed that they were able to loosen the thick ropes, and the wall was about to crumble, when right then Mr. Shimmel's Subaru screeched to a halt right next to us. The councilman got out of the car and raced over to the workers. "Stop immediately!" he said.

"Who are *you*?" they asked. He pulled out his

councilman's identity card, but they weren't impressed. "We only take orders from Oppenheimer," they told him.

"Wait," he said, and took a cellular phone out of his pocket, quickly punched in some numbers, and spoke a few words into it. We didn't hear what he said, but from the look on his face we could see that he was arguing with someone.

After a few minutes, he handed the phone to the work foreman who talked briefly with the man on the other end.

Then he closed the phone and with a disappointed expression said, "Okay men, time to quit."

The workers and supervisor disappeared as fast as they had come.

"Great job," I heard myself saying to Mr. Shimmel. Only then did he notice us. "So — you're the ones making all the trouble," he said and got into his car.

Tzviki kept us posted about the discussions in the City Council about whether or not to leave the structure standing. Several members of the Council said that the man who lived there might be dangerous and that children wouldn't be able to use the park's playground.

That wasn't true. Little kids were around there all the time and they just got used to the strange man among them. Some of the councilmen decided to go there to check it out for themselves. We found out about it through Mr. Shimmel, and that day practically the whole class went to play in the park's playground.

Actually, we were too old to play in the park. It felt really strange to go back to the slides and swings that we had practically forgotten how to use. But every so often we shot a glance in the direction of the group of big shots who were looking at us, and this made us play even harder. That evening, Mr. Shimmel told Tzviki's father, "The matter is settled. They all felt that the man is not dangerous. The demolition order has been canceled."

And that's what happened. Within a few days, the Cave Man started to build his "cave" again, and the children kept coming with their mothers to play in the playground. We used to pass by each day to see how the building (which, by the way, never stopped) was progressing and how the Cave Man felt.

One day, after school, I went to Struk Park by myself. I looked at the "fourth room" that the Cave Man had built. I looked for a long time, until I realized that someone was watching me.

It was the Cave Man.

He stood there on the other side of the "building" and stared at me. I didn't move from my place and I looked back at him. I watched as the expression on his face changed. At first, he looked at me as if he had spotted a familiar face. This expression turned to recognition. Yes, he recognized the boy who had come in his cave that Shabbos and had been so frightened of him. He apparently recognized the boy who used to run away from him every Shabbos after that. He made the connection between that same boy and the group of boys who had done so much for him, who had brought him all the building materials and who had stopped the destruction of his home.

For several long minutes we stared at each other, and then... He lifted his hand to his head and, with a strange gesture, took off his hat and bowed.

I nodded my head to him slightly. I felt that I had needed his forgiveness and that in those moments, I had received it.

Then he opened the large cardboard door of his cave, threw me one last look, and went inside.

Once again, he went back to being the Cave Man.

Shh – Someone's Listening!

My name is Gila. I'm eleven years old and I'm in the sixth grade.

I'm a pretty studious girl and very popular. Almost everyone is friends with me. Almost. Ruthi isn't my friend — since yesterday. I'll tell you why, even though it's very embarrassing.

Ruthi is a quiet, gentle girl. I was her friend for a long time. I knew she could be trusted and that I could count on her. Even though the other girls in the class didn't see that much in her, neither good nor bad, I found a lot of good things in her and I built the friendship between us.

Yesterday, Malki came to my house. She's full of energy and liked by the whole class. We did homework together, played and talked.

Suddenly I remembered that I had promised Ruthi that I would go over to her house. When I told Malki, she just shrugged and said, "I'm not planning on going with you."

"Then maybe we can ask her to come here," I suggested.

Malki wrinkled her nose. "Call her up and tell her you can't come."

I listened to her and made the phone call. I don't know why, I just did.

"Can I talk to Ruthi?" I asked when someone in Ruthi's house answered the phone. From the corner of my eye I saw Malki making a face and I almost burst out laughing.

"Hello?" I heard Ruthi's voice.

"I'm calling to let you know that I can't come," I said.

"Why not?" Ruthi asked.

"Because...um...because I don't feel good," I lied.

"Oh! I hope you feel better," Ruthi wished me and asked what hurt.

By now, I was already too much into the lie to think of a way to get out of it. "My ears hurt," I said, and almost exploded with laughter at the face Malki was making. All of a sudden I forgot about my close friendship with Ruthi. All of a sudden I ignored the prohibition against lying. I acted foolishly just to have fun.

I kept on lying and lying until the conversation ended with Ruthi's heartfelt wishes for my speedy recovery.

I put down the receiver, and Malki and I burst out laughing. We didn't notice that...

"How come you had to explain and apologize to her so much?" Malki asked scornfully.

I wanted to say that Ruthi was my very best friend, but I was embarrassed to say that to Malki. I was afraid she would think less of me for having Ruthi, who wasn't part of the "in" crowd, for a friend. That's why I said, "No special reason — I just wanted to be nice to her."

"What do you see in that quiet girl?" scoffed Malki.

"I'm trying to help her," I made up a new lie on the spot. "The poor thing has no friends and that's why I volunteered to be her friend."

And so the conversation continued, and, without my even noticing it, I found myself talking about my very best friend in a condescending, scornful manner. The conversation with Malki was full of gossip and slander, pure *lashon hara*. Why? All because I wasn't strong enough to say, "I'm her friend, and that's it."

The conversation continued for another half hour, and then suddenly we fell silent. That's when we heard a strange sound coming from the receiver. I picked it up and said hello. It was Ruthi's voice I heard. She sounded hurt and bitter.

"Gila," she said, "you forgot to hang up the

phone the right way. I'm sorry I listened in to your conversation, but I guess it was meant to be. Thanks for your good intentions, but I don't want any friends who feel sorry for me. So, I wish you all the best."

I stood there shocked. I wished the ground would open up and swallow me. I didn't say a thing. "Do you hear me?" Ruthi whispered into the phone.

"I hear you," I said. "Ruthi, I have to explain what happened—"

"There's no need to explain," Ruthi said, her voice shaking. She too was crying, just like I was. "There's no need for any explanation," she repeated. "You agree with me, don't you?"

All of a sudden I realized that there really wasn't anything to explain. I thought over the conversation between me and Malki and I knew that because of something stupid I had lost forever the very best and super most faithful friend I had ever had.

Now I'm sitting here in my room, alone. Sitting and remembering, ashamed and crying.

I learned a lot from this painful incident. I learned a lot about silliness, about gossip and slander. I realized that even if Ruthi wouldn't have heard the conversation, it would have still been heard in Heaven. Maybe, as I told Ruthi, it was "meant" for her to hear it so that I'd really feel how terrible it is to speak *lashon hara*.

I'm sitting here and crying. I wish Ruthi could know the truth. But how will she know if I don't tell her? I'll just have to get over the bad feelings. Still, it's hard to believe she'll forgive me.

What will happen to me? Will I ever find as good a friend again?

The Boy on Bus #37

My name is Micha'el and I'm twelve. I'm in the seventh grade and I live in Jerusalem in Rehavia.

The school I go to is in Geula and every day I go there on bus #37. The ride takes at least twenty minutes.

Most of my friends live in Geula. In my neighborhood there isn't even one boy who goes to my school besides me.

Because the bus is always so crowded, every day I have to give up my seat to elderly people. I know, it's a mitzvah to do what's written: "Stand before the elderly and give honor to the old." But besides the merit of the mitzvah, I also get a lot of compliments. "What a well brought up boy." And, "Where do you see children like that nowadays," etc. I sort of like compliments (actually, I'm not the only one).

Two weeks ago I got on the bus as usual and sat down in the second row. Opposite me sat a religious boy I didn't know. I didn't pay any attention to him. It can happen that someone I don't know gets on the bus.

The bus went along its route and got filled up until all the seats were taken.

And then an old lady carrying a shopping bag got on. Naturally, I rushed to stand up and offer her my seat. She nodded her head in thanks.

At the next stop, an elderly man got on. He looked around to find a seat. All the seats were taken by adults. Then his glance fell on the boy.

I was positive he would get up...but he didn't.

The elderly man looked at him, and I too tried to catch his eye, but he made out as if he didn't see anything. I saw that he felt uncomfortable, but, still, he didn't get up from his seat.

All around people started to comment: "Look at that boy. He sees that elderly gentleman quite well yet it doesn't even occur to him to get up."

The boy didn't budge from his place.

The other passengers started to speak up more loudly. "What chutzpah!" said one lady.

"Look how the religious educate their children," said another man.

I was burning mad at that boy. I couldn't understand it — how dare he act that way?

One younger passenger, who stood near me, said to the boy, "Tell me something, don't you see the elderly gentleman standing? Don't you have any respect? Don't you have any manners?"

The boy turned his face to the window, and to me it looked as if he didn't care and was trying to ignore what was going on.

The protests got louder, and then the young man next to me said to the boy, "Listen buddy, if you don't get up, I'll *make* you get up."

The boy burst out crying and stood up.

The next second all the passengers in the bus felt ashamed of themselves.

The boy started to move out of his place and you could see right away that he was handicapped.

He limped really badly. Slowly he made his way to the back door, when suddenly he tripped over a bag in the aisle and fell flat on his face.

Someone helped him get up. He looked miserable. "Sit down, sit down, we didn't know," said a passenger. The boy cried and said, "I don't need any favors. I'll go on another bus."

The bus stopped at a bus stop, and the boy shuffled to the door in a way that made your heart go out to him. Not only did he limp, but one arm was paralyzed, making it hard for him to manage.

The bus continued on its route. All the passengers looked at the boy standing there at the bus stop, crying. His place remained empty. No one dared sit in it. The young man who had shouted at him and embarrassed him lowered his head in shame. Each person on the bus felt that he was slightly to blame. Even I.

I came home sad. I kept on thinking about that boy.

I told my mother the story. You could see she hadn't heard a story like that before. Although she reassured me that I wasn't to blame, because I hadn't hurt his feelings but had only thought badly of him, I still felt bad.

My father said, "Look how important it is to judge a person favorably." He said it over and over again and then pointed out that he was repeating it not just for my benefit, but for his own.

"I probably would have thought the same thing you did about the boy," said my father. "Even worse, I probably would have told him to get up from his seat. Now, after you told me this story, I'll be extra careful before I rebuke someone."

Two weeks passed.

Yesterday, as usual, I got on the bus after school, glanced around to look for a seat...

And suddenly I saw him.

At first I was very surprised, but then I felt really happy that I would finally have a chance to apologize to him for the embarrassment he had gone through.

I sat down next to him. I felt uncomfortable about starting a conversation, but I decided to do it anyway, so I asked him his name.

"Chezi," he answered.

I asked him where he lived. It turned out that he lived in Rehavia, too, but went to a different school. After all the usual questions, we were silent, and then I got up the courage to say, "Listen, once I was...on a bus...when they shouted at you...and I'm really sorry...that I didn't stand up for you. I didn't know, I just didn't know that..."

The boy smiled and said, "It happens to me sometimes. Not exactly that way, though, that someone threatens to pick me up by force, but sometimes I hear a lot of grumbling and complaining. My mother explained to me that they just don't know that I'm handicapped. Until about a month ago we lived in a different place, where I didn't need the bus so much, and besides that, I had crutches and everyone could see that I couldn't get up. Now I don't have any crutches, it makes me a few problems..."

He stopped and smiled because he understood what he was saying. A kid's supposed to be happy that he doesn't have crutches, but for him, it made "a few problems."

The bus pulled up to the bus stop. A few elderly people got on. I rushed to give up my seat to one old man, and right after that another old man came over expecting Chezi to get up.

Chezi looked at me pleadingly. I saw that he expected me to get him out of the predicament.

It was hard to find the right words, but I decided that I had to try. "Excuse me, Sir, that boy can't get up." I took a deep breath and added, "He's handicapped, he can't stand up...."

The man smiled apologetically. "I understand. It's okay, don't worry about it."

During the rest of the ride I had to say that sentence a few more times. People accepted it with understanding, and everyone sent a smile of encouragement to the boy.

We got to Rehavia. Chezi had to get off at the stop before mine. I decided to get off with him and walk the rest of the way by foot. We talked for a while. I found out that he finished school at different hours than I did and that we couldn't ride the bus together except for twice a week. We made up between us that at least those two times I would go with him.

This story is not yet over. Chezi became my friend. He's a smart kid, and clever too, and the fact that he's handicapped doesn't bother me at all. Probably next year he'll transfer to my school and that'll make it easier for both of us.

I'm learning a lot from Chezi. But the most important thing I learned since meeting him is: "Judge everyone favorably."

The Quiet and the Storm

My name is Shuki. I live in Haifa and I'm in the eighth grade. A week ago I celebrated my bar mitzvah.

I have an amazing story that I want to tell you (it could be that you already heard this story because it was in the newspapers).

But before that, I want to tell you about myself. Maybe that will interest you, too.

If you'd ask what kind of student I am, it would be hard to give you an answer — it depends on a few things. First of all, it depends on what row I'm sitting in, and also who my teacher is, what kind of beard and lips he has, and if he talks precisely or not.

Does all this sound strange to you? It's the truth, though. There were years when I got excellent grades and my behavior was the best, and there were years when I was considered a trouble-maker who didn't know a thing about what was studied in class.

It's time to tell you — it's related to my problem: I have a hearing disability. I wear two hearing aids, one behind each ear. You've probably seen these things that go on the ears right about where a lot of kids loop their *peyos*.

A few months after I was born, my parents noticed that I didn't react to any sounds. A series of tests confirmed their fears. "Your son is probably deaf," they were told. My parents didn't know how to cope with this tragedy (that's what they told me years later.) All of a sudden they needed to find solutions for things they had considered the simplest things in the world until then.

But my parents are special. They put all their efforts into me. To their great relief, it turned out that I wasn't completely deaf, but could hear some sounds and noises. They thanked God for this gift and decided to take advantage of it to help me make as much progress as possible.

You may not know it, but lots of deaf people find it very hard to talk. After all, how can a person learn to talk if he can't hear? Even those who do learn to talk don't say the letters the right way because they can't hear themselves and they can't distinguish, for instance, between the letter "p" and "b". That's why we sometimes say, "I want to blay."

My parents worked hard so that I'd be able to pronounce words as much as possible the right way. And they succeeded.

I've always gone to a regular school and I've never had any problems with friends. I must say that the kids in my class treat me just like a regular kid, and even better. They're just great.

But school work? Here's where my problems begin. The hearing aids only help to increase the strength of the sound waves around me, but their help is not enough. Try swimming underwater in a pool and shouting to a friend — will he hear you? That's about what the sounds I hear are like. Do I make myself clear?

In order to understand what people are saying, I have to read their lips, that is, to constantly look at their mouth while they talk. The combination of faint noises and lip movements lets me understand what's being said.

Over time, I learned to "lip-read" perfectly. It even gives me an advantage over hearing kids. I can "read" a conversation that's taking place at the other end of an auditorium (because my sight is fabulous, thank God). But here's where the problem starts.

When I had teachers who spoke distinctly, with strong and clear lip movements, it was easy for me to pay attention to what was said, and then I was a good student. But it sometimes happened that I had teachers whose lip movements were weak, or whose lips hardly moved. Another problem I have – and this may make you laugh, but it isn't funny to me at all – is that there are also teachers who talk pretty clearly, I guess, but their mustaches hide their lips, making it very hard, and sometimes impossible, for me to read their lips.

There was one teacher (whom I really liked), that the day he got a haircut was a holiday for me, because the barber would trim his mustache in a way that didn't hide his lips, and then I was able to pay attention the way I should.

With the others, though, I didn't have that luck. Imagine how I felt inside. Imagine how bitter I felt knowing that all because of lip movements that were too fast or a mustache that was too long I couldn't understand a thing!

I want you to know that it's much harder for me to concentrate in class than it is for other kids, but if I have a rebbe who tries to make it easier for me, I try very hard to pay attention and to be a good student.

When you have the will power, you succeed.

The best proof of how will power works is the fact that I managed to read the *haftarah* at my bar mitzvah with the *ta'amei hamikra* (I'm not sure you understand how hard that is for someone with a hearing disability).

Actually, until about half a year ago I was positive that I wouldn't read the Torah on my bar mitzvah Shabbos.

What changed my mind was something that happened then, and that's what I'm going to tell you.

It all started when I got a telescope for my twelfth birthday.

A telescope is like binoculars, but much more powerful. If you look through it at trees that are far away, they look close up and huge. I like to go up on the roof of our house and look through my telescope at the ships anchored in the Haifa port. I like to watch the row boats bringing crew members to the ships anchored in the middle of the sea. I even recognize some of them from their previous visits. I can clearly see the name of each boat, which is usually painted on its side.

One day an aircraft carrier arrived in the port. Its name was *Eisenhower*.

I used to watch it for hours. It was amazing. Dozens of planes were parked on it. Some of them took off and landed on the ship. It was hard to believe, but I saw it with my own eyes. The ship looked more like a floating island, like a city on the sea, than a ship.

The incident I want to tell you about happened three days after the ship arrived. It was early in the evening when there was still some light left. Through the telescope I followed a boat that left the ship for the port. I saw how it anchored. A few dozen sailors got off, and a few dozen boarded.

After a quarter of an hour, it left the port and went back.

The sea was stormy. I knew it even without the telescope because of the white froth on the Kiryat Chaim beach, on the other shore of the bay. The telescope also gave me a clear view of the boats rocking in the waves. The *Eisenhower*, on the other hand, was completely calm, as if what was happening in the water had nothing to do with it.

I kept my eyes on the boat bringing the sailors back to their ship. It was a regular trip. I had already seen hundreds like it.

The boat left the port and started to make its way in the open sea. I focused the telescope on it and immediately realized that it was in trouble.

It spun around and around in a circle. I saw it was tipped to the side. I could see sailors running on the deck. It was obvious to me that something out of the ordinary was going on.

The first thing I did was to go down from

the roof to the house and take the cordless phone back up with me — just to have it.

I went back to the telescope, pointed it, and when I looked through the lens again, I saw the boat laying on its side.

I turned the telescope to the *Eisenhower* and from there to the port. There was no sign of any activity. I realized that no one knew what had happened.

I dialed 100.

I waited a few seconds. Naturally, I didn't hear any dialing sounds (you probably forgot about my problem, because of the drama. But I live with it.)

Usually, when someone picks up a receiver, there's a noise that helps me realize that the other side has picked up the phone. When I heard the "click" I started to talk fast into the receiver: "Hello, my name is Shuki Levy. I'm deaf and will not be able to hear what you answer. Please listen to me. I am looking through a telescope at the port. There is an overturned boat there. There are sailors in the water. It is completely upside-down. No one is coming to help. Do you hear me? Get help. I am watching through a telescope. If you need any help, call this number...."

I hung up and looked at the boat. It was

slowly sinking. Sailors were in the water around it. No help had come yet.

All of a sudden the port burst into life. Dozens of motor boats left the port and nearby ships all at once. I was very excited. I felt my whole body tremble. Every few minutes I glanced at the phone to see if the light was flashing (the flashing light signals a call).

The light flashed.

I pressed the button. Of course, I didn't hear anything, but I shouted into the receiver: "It's me, Shuki. I can't hear you, but I can tell you what I see. I have a very good telescope. There are a few motor boats over there and they are surrounding the boat. You should send some divers because there are a few dozen sailors hanging on the boat, and another ten floating in the water. Besides that, radio the green boat to go in the direction of Kiryat Chaim. I can spot someone there with white clothes fighting the waves. If you are in communication with them, tell them now, okay?"

I looked through the telescope and saw the green boat start to go off in the direction of Kiryat Chaim.

"More to the right," I shouted.

A few seconds passed. It moved right.

"Now straight, a little bit left. That's it. He made it to him." The sailor was rescued.

That's how one of the strangest rescue operations in history took place. A boy of twelve with a hearing impairment ran a whole naval rescue operation by phone to the police station and from there to the rescuers.

A funny thought did occur to me that maybe I was only imagining that the boats were doing what I had instructed and that I was really talking with my aunt in Rehovot who didn't know what I wanted. But I ignored that humiliating thought and did what I could.

I must have been talking on the phone non-stop for an hour, without knowing if they heard me or not.

Then it got dark, and I told them I was sorry, but I couldn't see a thing. Naturally, I didn't hear any answer, and hung up.

That night the police came to our house. A tall man stood in the doorway and told my parents what had happened. It turns out that this policemen had heard me the whole time and had acted according to my instructions. When I called, a policewoman had answered. At first she thought someone was playing a trick, but something in my voice made her call the coast guard. They tried to make contact with the boat, but couldn't.

The call that came after that was from the coast guard. They broadcast my voice through loudspeakers all over their base, and acted according to what I reported.

It turns out that I helped a lot because the boats at the site couldn't see what I saw. Only when a few helicopters were brought in did they not need me any more. They tried to tell me that on the phone, but I, of course, couldn't hear, and continued to talk, and that's why they took me off the speakers and just the one policewoman kept on listening, to be polite.

Late that night, the American captain of the ship came. I was already asleep. He thanked my parents warmly. He said that thanks to me thirty-seven American sailors were saved. He added, that to everyone's great sorrow, another seven had drowned. The captain explained that if another few minutes had gone by, the number of those who drowned would have been much greater, and that thanks to my call for help and directions before the helicopters arrived, dozens of people were saved.

He gave my parents an invitation, especially for them and me, to come and visit the ship.

The next day the story was all over the newspapers in Israel and the rest of the world. When I got to school, my friends already knew all the details.

At first I felt a little uncomfortable with all the fuss being made, but after that I decided that I had done a service to all the other people and kids who are deaf. People should know that we're no less talented than everyone else, and that our disability doesn't prevent us from doing what has to be done. I was happy that the newspapers made note of the way I had overcome my handicap. I knew that a lot of deaf people and those with hearing impairments would be reading it and that they'd be encouraged.

A week later we went to visit the ship. We got there by helicopter. It was a lot of fun, but it was only the beginning of what awaited us on the ship itself. We were greeted like royalty. All the ship's crew stood on deck and saluted us, and we're talking about, just so you know, 3000 people. After a short tour of the ship, we all went into a huge auditorium and there the captain gave a long speech. I watched his lips but didn't understand a word. He spoke in English.

After that the coast guard captain spoke, the one who listened to me for half an hour on the speaker and acted according to my instructions. Since he spoke in Hebrew, there was a translator standing next to him to translate what he said into English for the ship's crew members.

He told the whole story to the sailors. Every so often I saw everyone rolling with laughter.

After that he looked at me and must have been talking to me. Everyone looked at me with admiration. I figured out that he must be praising me a lot. Even though he spoke in Hebrew, I didn't understand a word he said.

Listen, if you would have seen the thick mustache he had, you would have understood why....

Kiddush Levana

My name is Motti. I'm in the fifth grade.

I'm a little chubby, and am considered a very popular kid.

My story is named "*Kiddush Levana*" (the blessing over the New Moon) because it starts and ends with that same blessing that people say once a month at the end of Shabbos, outside shul, facing the moon.

You all probably know about that prayer. Everyone finishes Ma'ariv, then takes a special large plastic "*Kiddush Levana*" bentcher, says the blessing and then says "*Shalom Aleichem*" to three different people. Each one responds, "*Aleichem Shalom.*" At the end of the short prayer everyone sings and dances "*Tovim Me'orot*" to the familiar tune you're probably thinking of right now.

At the end of the blessing, some people, instead of returning the *bentchers* to where they belong in shul, shove them into the hands of children standing nearby. The problem is, some kids — including me — are too lazy to put them back inside. But because we're only children and we have to respect our elders, even if we're too lazy, we have no choice but to take the *bentchers*. In my heart, though, I always promise myself that when I grow up, I won't act that way.

It was *motzai Shabbos* after *Rosh Chodesh* Kislev. The *Kiddush Levana* blessing was said as usual. When it was over, the adults rushed to give me and my friends the *bentchers*.

All of a sudden I thought of what seemed like a cute trick. I took my *bentchers* and collected all the others from my friends as well, and hid both my hands filled with the *bentchers* behind my back. Then I went over to Zevi, my friend, who goes to the same shul as I do.

"I have a surprise for you!" I told him.

His face lit up. "What's the surprise?" he asked.

"Guess," I said.

"A chocolate bar? Candy?" he tried to guess.

"No, no, and no," I said. "Much, much more..."

His face took on an eager expression. "Gimme."

"Close your eyes and hold out your hands."

Zevi closed his eyes tightly, stretched out his hands and waited expectantly. I, of course, put the pile of bentchers on them and ran away to the sound of the laughter of the rest of the kids, who had done just what I did.

Zevi was left standing there all by himself. When he opened his eyes and saw the "surprise" he had anticipated, and saw how I had "gotten" him, his face filled with humiliation and rage.

His first reaction was to run after me, to give me back the unexpected "present," but I raced away and he found it hard to run because of the load of bentchers he was carrying.

When he saw he couldn't catch me, he made his way back to the shul and put all the bentchers in their place. After a few minutes I saw him leaving, looking sad, embarrassed, and very, very angry.

The instant he spotted me, he started to chase after me. When he saw that he couldn't catch up he shouted, "I'm never going to talk to you again!"

I didn't pay any attention to what he said. But the next day when I got to school I saw that he was ignoring me completely. He didn't try to yell at me and didn't even try to get back at me. He just ignored me.

It stayed that way for the rest of the day and the next day, too. Zevi just ignored my very existence. He treated me as if I were invisible.

It didn't take long before the rest of the class caught on. They all knew that "Zevi was mad at Motti." It made me very unhappy. Sometimes fights can happen, but to be mad at someone is something else. When two kids argue, or even fight, it's not nice — but it's over in a day. But being mad is more serious and permanent and can get worse with time.

I was really worried about it, but even though I knew for sure that I was the one who should go and talk to him, my pride wouldn't let me.

During the coming weeks, all the kids in the class knew never to put us on the same team, and of course, never to mention the name of one in the presence of the other. There were a few kids who tried to heat up the fight between us. Others tried to get us to make up, but with no results. Zevi didn't even want to hear about me, he was so hurt by how I'd tricked him.

It's not easy to be fighting with a friend. Believe me, it's no fun to know that someone in the world thinks badly of you.

A month passed. It was the saddest and

most difficult month in my whole life. All of a sudden I was forced to deal with things I'd never faced before, and worst of all, I knew that I was to blame.

Rosh Chodesh Tevet arrived. On the following *motzai Shabbos,* all the people in shul went outside for *Kiddush Levana.* I said the prayer and I remembered what had happened exactly a month before. I remembered that the month before, instead of praying that "my enemies won't be able to harm me" I had been busy planning a trick that humiliated one of my best friends. "That's the reason that instead of dancing, I was sad all this month," I thought. I decided then and there that I had to find a solution to this fight. I couldn't keep going on this way.

But what could I do?

I continued saying *Kiddush Levana.* When I got to *Shalom Aleichem,* I went over to my father. "*Shalom Aleichem,*" I said.

"*Aleichem Shalom,*" he answered.

I went over to my big brother Elazar. "*Shalom Aleichem.*"

"*Aleichem Shalom.*"

That was two — there was only one more person to say it to. I realized what I had to do.

I looked through the crowd for Zevi and

found him right away. I started to make my way towards him. He noticed me coming. I stood in front of him without saying a thing.

At first, he pretended that he was still praying, but my firm stance made it clear that I wanted to say something to him. He lifted his head from the *Siddur* and looked at me.

There was a moment's silence. It took a lot of courage for me to say, "*Shalom Aleichem.*"

Silence.

Tension.

"*Aleichem Shalom,*" I heard him say, and a huge stone rolled off my heart.

"Yay!" we heard shouts of amazement from all our friends who knew about our fight.

When the prayers were over, Meir, a nice, friendly kid, came over to me.

"Close your eyes," he said. "I have a surprise for you."

"You don't have to," I told him. I reached behind his back, took the pile of bentchers he was holding, went over to Zevi, took his too, and went into the shul.

It was so easy, that I decided right then and there to take it upon myself to do that job from then on.

"*Tovim me'orot,*" the congregation started to sing and dance. I joined the circle. I wasn't alone.

Glasses

My name is Ari. I'm writing this during recess. I didn't go out. I'm writing you a small story.

I live in Jerusalem.

I'm an average kid, medium tall. I have a lot of friends, and I never had any special problems — except for one, and it's one that I brought on myself. That's what I'm going to write about now.

One day, one of the kids in my class, Motti's his name, complained that he couldn't see what was written on the blackboard. The teacher took a piece of paper and wrote a note to his parents: "Please take Motti for an eye examination. He complains that he can't see what's written on the blackboard."

Motti folded the note and looked very pleased. Naturally — he had suddenly become important.

The teacher then asked, "Are there any other children who can't see well?"

Yossi raised his hand and after that Akiva did too. Yanky, the quietest boy in the class, also raised his hand.

All of a sudden I decided that I couldn't see well either. Don't ask me why. I just raised my hand.

Here's where I want to tell you something.

Kids like glasses. I don't know why, maybe because not everyone has glasses, maybe because it makes them look big. I don't know what the exact reason is, but the fact is that in their heart of hearts most kids want glasses. Sure it's ridiculous. But sometimes kids do stupid things, 'cause they're kids.

And that's exactly what I did — something stupid. I "decided" that I "couldn't see well." I raised my hand confidently. The teacher called me up to his desk after Yanky and before Yossi. He asked me, "Can you see what's written there on the poster to your right?"

Naturally I answered no.

I got the treasured note and waited impatiently for school to end. I imagined how I'd go with my mother to the eye doctor and how he'd decide that I needed glasses, and how I'd go back to school with some beautiful glasses with gold frames. Actually, I thought, round glasses made out of plastic like Shimmy's suited me better. I couldn't decide. But I felt as if they were going to buy me a new bike. Go ahead and laugh, but that's how I felt.

I got home, and here's where I had a little problem. I always tell my mother the truth. I never lie to her. I was afraid to do it now. That's why I just handed her the teacher's note. She read it and then took the "Masoret" book that my little brother was learning the Hebrew alphabet from, opened it to a page where all the letters were written big, and started to test me.

"What letter is this?" she asked.

"I can't see," I answered.

"And this?"

"I can't see."

She turned the page to where the letters were even bigger.

"This?"

"I don't know."

"And this?"

"I can't see."

Imma put the book down and said, "Your teacher was smart to notice. We're going to the eye doctor today."

We went.

The uncomfortable feeling bothering me disappeared. I told myself, "After all, the teacher himself wrote that I don't see well, and my mother also said that we have to go to the eye doctor, so I guess I really don't see well." I just convinced myself that I needed glasses.

We arrived at the eye doctor's clinic. He put some special glasses on me, put lenses in them and asked me, "Can you see anything?"

"No."

He changed the lenses and asked, "And now?"

"No."

"You may need a higher number," the doctor said. (Now I was really convinced that I had a problem. After all, even the doctor said so!)

The doctor put in a higher number and then said, "Now it's good."

He started to ask me all the letters and numbers that were on the chart in front of me and I read them off one after the other without any problem. The doctor said, "Good. That's the number you need. Now you may leave the room so that I can speak with your mother."

I left and waited expectantly.

After a few minutes, my mother came out. I asked her tensely, "What did he say, Imma?"

"That we have to buy glasses."

I wanted to jump for joy, but I pretended to be upset. "Ugh, glasses," I said.

"Don't worry," my mother consoled me. "It's hard at first, and you might feel dizzy, but you'll get used to it in the end."

"Um, Imma — will we go buy them now?"

"We'll see," she said. "If it's open."

I prayed that the optician would be open.
And he was.

We went in. My mother began to put different frames on me and ask me if I liked them.
After about ten minutes, we chose some fabulous frames. They were round, and made out of
black plastic. I liked them a lot. I felt like a
professor in them.

My mother gave the frames to the salesman,
gave him the doctor's note, and he said, "Fine.
Come in tomorrow."

My good mood evaporated in an instant.
"No, Imma," I whispered to her. "I want them
today."

"What's the rush?" she asked me calmly.
"Tomorrow after school we'll go and get them."

Imma began to walk towards the exit. I
started to cry from disappointment. "Imma,
talk to him. I want the glasses today."

Imma thought for a minute and all of a sudden an idea occurred to her. "Wait here," she
said. "I'll go talk to him."

I was left standing next to the display window. I saw her talking with the salesman. She
explained something to him with a lot of hand
motions. She nodded her head to me to signal
that he agreed. After that, he disappeared into
his workroom. I waited anxiously. My mother

called me into the store. A while later, the optician came out of his room with a case in one hand and...glasses in the other. He placed the glasses in the case and said, "That's it."

My mother paid him. We went out of the store. I told my mother that I wanted to wear them. She said, "Wait until we get home," but I insisted. So right there, in the middle of the sidewalk, she took the glasses out of their case and put them on me.

I was flying. I was so happy. My mother asked me, "Well, how do you see?" Naturally I answered her that I could see great. My mother pointed to different signs and I read them all easily. She didn't seem as happy as I was. I figured it was hard for her to accept the fact that her son needed glasses.

That night I practically fell asleep with the glasses. A second before I fell asleep I took them off and put them in the case. I found it hard to fall asleep. Finally I fell asleep with great expectations for the next day, when I would show off my glasses to my friends.

I woke up early in the morning. Naturally, right after I washed my hands for the morning I put on my glasses. I got dressed fast, drank a cup of cocoa, grabbed the snack my mother had prepared and was about to run out the front door and off to school.

That's when my mother said to me, "Ari, are you sure you can see well?"

"Sure," I said. "I can see perfectly."

"It doesn't seem to you that he prepared the lenses in too much of a rush?" she asked.

"You're just worrying for nothing," I reassured her. "I really see great. You can test me," I added.

Imma took the Masoret book with the big letters, stood a few steps away from me and started to ask me.

I saw the letters easily and even said the name of each and every letter that Imma pointed to. She turned to the page where the letters were printed smaller. I was also able to read them very easily. After that, she turned to the really small letters. I was able to read these too, with no trouble at all.

Imma ended the "exam" and closed the book. I said, "Imma, I'm in a hurry. Bye."

"Why are you in such a hurry?" she said. "It's only 7:30."

"I want to get to *cheder* fast to show... Imma, what happened to you? Why are you so sad?"

Imma didn't answer. She sat in the chair looking very miserable.

"What happened, Imma?" I asked again. Something was wrong, but I didn't know what.

"My son doesn't tell the truth. Why shouldn't I be sad?"

I didn't say anything.

"Listen to me, Ari," said Imma. "Yesterday, when we were in the store, you really wanted the glasses right away. I couldn't stand firm in the face of your begging, and I told the salesman that he should take the measurements for the frame and prepare the new lenses for tomorrow. In the meantime..."

"In the meantime what?" I heard myself say.

"In the meantime he put regular glass into the frames. Plain glass, without any number, so that you'd feel good. Do you understand what I am saying? Do you know what this means?"

Of course I knew what it meant. How embarrassing. How humiliating. I couldn't look my mother in the eyes. I couldn't think about the fact that from the moment we left the store and I read all the street signs with no problem, my mother already knew I didn't need glasses. And the proof: I saw fine through the plain glass that had no number.

My mother talked with me a little. I won't repeat the details of that conversation. It was important to her that I shouldn't feel bad about being caught, but about the fact that I had tried to get something through deceit. She also explained to me that if the lie wouldn't have been found out, I would have suffered a lot more. My eyes would have been ruined, and the lie would have been revealed. And not only my mother would have known, but all the kids in class. Imma explained to me that I should be happy that Hashem made things turn out that the truth was discovered at an early stage, to prevent me from suffering and shame.

I was late for school. My mother gave me a note. It didn't say, "...through no fault of his own...." Imma wrote the teacher that I was late because she had a conversation with me, after which it became clear that I didn't need glasses.

The teacher read the note, looked at me for a minute, and then laughed a friendly laugh, clapped me on my shoulder and said, "Sit down, Ari. You're lucky that your mother 'sees' better than you do."

Now I'm sitting here during recess writing this story so that at least you will not even think about trying to get glasses if you don't need them. Anyone who does, will be, at the best, really embarrassed, and at the worst — he'll also be embarrassed, plus he'll need...a pair of glasses for the eyes he ruined.

The Last Letter

My name is Yonatan. I live in Haifa and I'm in the second grade.

If you don't like sad stories then please don't read my story. It's sad.

I have a sister named Channi. She's in the seventh grade. Channi has a friend named Shoshanna who lives in a moshav near Haifa. They both go to the same school.

A year ago, when I was in the first grade, Shoshanna came to visit us in our house. She saw me and asked me what grade I was in. I told her and she said, "Great! You're the same age as my brother Nachum. You can be pen pals with him."

I didn't know what a pen pal was. My sister explained to me that it means you send letters and get letters back. It meant that Shoshanna wanted me to write letters to Nachum and he would send me letters back.

"But I don't know your brother Nachum," I said.

Shoshanna and my sister explained to me that I didn't have to know him before I wrote to him. "You'll get to know him through the letters and he'll get to know you. You'll tell him all about yourself, and he'll tell you about himself."

The idea sounded good to me. I agreed, and Shoshanna explained to me how to send a letter. She told me the name of their street and the house number and taught me how to write: "Mr. Nachum Yaslovitz." She showed me how to write it on the smooth side of the envelope, and how to write my name and address on the back flap, the "tongue." I liked the idea of the "tongue."

The very next day I took a pencil and paper and started to write a letter. "My name is Yonatan Levy," I wrote. "You have probably heard about me from your sister. It's a little strange for me to write to a boy I never saw, but at least through the letters we can get to know each other. First of all, I'll tell you about myself. I'm in..."

It took me a while to write the letter. Maybe even a whole hour. I looked it over to make sure it was written in nice handwriting. I erased all the mistakes, and at the end, signed my name. I stuck a stamp on it and ran to the mail box at the end of the block.

I waited a day, two days, and when I didn't get an answer, I asked my sister to call the post office to ask what was going on. She laughed and said that the letter would reach Nachum only the next week and that it would take a few more days until he sent me a reply.

I waited impatiently. Every day when I came home from Talmud Torah, the first thing I would ask was, "Did the letter come?" Every day I was disappointed all over again.

But it finally came, after a week. My sister handed it to me as soon as I came home. Shoshanna had given her the letter. I raced to my room, opened it eagerly and started to read.

"I was very happy to get your letter," wrote Nachum. "I also like the idea. I'm also in the first grade." (We were still in the first grade then.) "Every day I travel an hour to get to my school, and also an hour back. That's why I am pretty tired when I come home from school. Anyway, the day I got your letter I sat down to write this letter."

Nachum went on to tell me about himself, and at the end of the long letter he suggested that we send our letters through our sisters to save the cost of the stamps. I was amazed that I hadn't thought of it. Actually, the whole idea of being pen pals was very new to me.

Our letter writing continued.

In the next letter I asked him why he had to travel a whole hour and he explained to me that his father was a teacher in a school far away, and that because he was so close to his father, and it was hard for him to study in the school in his moshav, it was decided that he would go to the school where his father taught. Nachum told me about the beautiful scenery he saw every day and about the traffic jams they sometimes got caught in, and I told him about what went on in Haifa, about my friends, about games, and everything.

As time went on, I began to realize that I had a good friend. Maybe even the best friend I ever had. I noticed that there wasn't any other friend I talked with about the things Nachum and I talked about in our letters. As the weeks and months went by, I decided that Nachum was a much more interesting boy than the boys in my class. At that point I began to imagine how he looked. Once I imagined that he was tall, and another time that he was short. Once I pictured him with dark hair, and another time, with blond hair. I really wanted to see him. Here I had a good friend and I didn't even know what he looked like!

Do you know what I mean?

I wrote him about it. "Nachum, don't you think the time has come for us to meet? We've been pen pals for almost a year. According to my calculations, I've written you seventeen letters, and now I'm writing the eighteenth. I don't know what you look like, and you don't know how I look, either. Maybe we should meet some time?"

The answer was not long in coming. "I was thinking exactly the same thing. The time has surely come, but I don't know how to get to your house and when. Do you have any suggestions?"

I did have a suggestion. "You can travel with your sister, Shoshanna," I wrote him. "Come after school and we can play until it's nighttime. Then your sister will take you home."

Our sisters were brought into the picture. It turned out that there was a problem. They both went to school in Haifa but Nachum went to school in a distant moshav and came home at about two o'clock. How could she take him if she was at school in Haifa?

We found a solution. Shoshanna would go home, pick up Nachum, and then come back with him to Haifa so that we could meet. It was pretty complicated, but when you really, really want something, it's like they say, "nothing stands in the way of will power."

I thought to myself, "That Shoshanna is really something. Look how she's willing to go to so much trouble for her brother." I wrote that to Nachum, and he told me a lot of good things about his sister.

We set a date for the meeting on the fourteenth of Sivan — another ten days. I counted the hours and days impatiently. I sent a letter to Nachum and wrote in it that I was really waiting and curious, too. He wrote me back that at nights he could hardly sleep a wink.

He asked me to write him again, before the meeting. I started to write a letter, but got a little lazy. I finished it a day before the meeting. I decided to hand it to him when we met.

And then the big day arrived.

I went to school without really wanting to. I counted the hours left until the end of classes. I was really nervous. I looked forward to the meeting more than anything.

School ended. I raced home, threw my bookbag down and ran straight to the window so that I'd be able to see Nachum when he came.

At two o'clock, Imma told me that my lunch was getting cold. I ate fast and ran back to the window.

My sister came and told me that Shoshanna had gone home and that within an hour and a half she would appear along with Nachum. I had never waited so hard for anything before. I kept looking at my watch. I pestered my sister with questions. "When will he come already? When will he come?" She was starting to get mad at me.

Three o'clock came and went, and so did four. My sister started to become impatient. "It's very strange," she said. "They should have been here at 3:30." Now she stood looking out the window, too.

At five, my sister called Nachum's house. There was no answer. "They're probably on their way," she said.

Six came and then seven. I started to cry. "They just promised but they didn't do what they said they would," I said sadly. My sister was pretty mad too, but she didn't say anything.

At 7:00, my mother called again, to see what was happening. I stood next to her when she talked on the phone. She spoke quietly, and suddenly I heard her shout, "Killed???"

I looked at her. I didn't know what to think. She started to cry. She ended the conversation quickly and looked at me.

"What happened?" I asked her.

My mother looked at me, her eyes filled with tears. She bit her lips, trying to control her emotions. She looked shocked.

"Your friend...went to school this morning, and...there was a crash and...he was hurt...very badly hurt...," my mother said.

"Was he killed?" I asked.

Imma didn't answer.

"Was he killed?" I asked again.

Imma nodded her head.

I didn't say anything. I went to my room, closed the door and didn't know what to think. I didn't even cry. It was like a nightmare. How could it be that I had waited for Nachum, with whom I had been pen pals for almost a whole year, and he had been killed? Killed means he died.

How could it be?

I can't tell you any more about how I felt that day and the following weeks. I had a lot of bad thoughts, frightening ones, like that it would happen to me, too. I was sad, and I didn't talk much. Abba and Imma talked to me all the time. They told me that I had to let go of what I had in my heart. I tried.

It wasn't easy. I told my father and mother a few times that they should leave me alone and that I didn't want to talk about this pain. My father explained to me that if I didn't take the pain out, it would stay inside me.

The pain did stay inside me. And not only

the pain. I kept thinking all the time about a subject that children don't usually think about much — death. Every kid knows that it exists, but when it happens right next to you, you can't not think about it.

My father decided to talk to me. "Just listen. If you can't answer, don't answer," he said.

My Father's Story

My father told me about his being an orphan. I knew that my father had been orphaned of his mother when he was my age. I had never asked him about it because the subject didn't concern me. For some reason, it didn't seem that sad to me, because my father was older and strong. But now he sat and told me what he had felt then. He described, first of all, himself.

"Yes, I was a tall, strong boy, but I was a child. The tragedy affected me deeply. It's hard for a child to deal with separations, especially if it's forever. There were days when I was so sad, so discouraged, that I just didn't have the desire to go to school and study.

"Sometimes I would get up at night, go to my mother's bed, lift up the cover and shout, 'Imma, Imma, where are you? Why did you leave me?' and cry."

I felt my eyes fill with tears. My father's

eyes filled with tears, too.

"One of those nights," my father continued to tell me, "my father woke up from my shouts and decided to talk to me. He told me, 'Your mother is here. You can't see her, because she is in Heaven, but Heaven is everywhere. Now she is looking at you and me, listening to what we are saying and—'

" 'Imma sees and hears me now?' I interrupted him.

" 'Yes, of course.'

" 'So why doesn't she answer me?'

"'She does answer you, but just in different ways. The World-to-Come is not the same as our world. It is a world where there's no need to eat, drink, or talk.'

" 'Then how do people understand each other?'

" 'It's here in this world that it's hard to understand one another. Not everyone knows how to express himself, and the relationship between people is not always as it should be. There, in that world, they understand without talking, through feeling. There are no fights there, no jealousy or hatred, and there is no misery there. Your mother is very happy there, and I think it's very important for her that you know this.'

"'How can I know this?'

" 'Close your eyes and imagine that she is telling it to you.'

"I closed my eyes," my father said, "and suddenly I imagined my mother smiling at me. It was such a relaxed and happy smile, and she said a lot, without words. I saw her in my imagination looking at me happily, with end-less love, and suddenly I opened my eyes and saw my father smiling."

"'Well?' he asked.

"'It's okay,' I heard myself say. 'I think I feel better.'

"From then on until today I live with com-plete acceptance of my mother's death. Yes, I still miss her, but at least I know that every-thing is good for her, and that she is really with me. The truth is, that I feel this many times. When things are difficult for me or sad for all kinds of reasons, I close my eyes, and she appears and calms me. Do the same thing, and you'll see that it's true."

My father finished his story, stroked my cheek gently and left the room.

I closed my eyes and tried to picture Nachum. Even though I had never seen his face, I had no trouble imagining it. I pictured a boy with fine features, smiling at me as if to say, "It's okay, Yonatan. Nothing happened to me. Everything's fine for me now. I'm in Gan Eden." I kept imagining it over and over again.

After a few minutes, I left my room. I knew that despite the pain I felt about Nachum's death, I would be strong. Something inside me told me that it was good for him there, and that this was what had been determined from Above. I had no right to grumble about it.

You could call my thought one simple word, "Faith" — Faith that everything that happens in the world is God's Will, and that God never does anything that doesn't need to be.

After a month, on the thirtieth day, I asked my father if I could go to Nachum's memorial service.

I saw my father's expression grow stern and I rushed to reassure him. "Don't worry, it's all right. I just want to visit him, to see where he's buried. Nothing will happen to me."

On the thirtieth day, I went up to Nachum's fresh grave. A small gravestone was there. I said *Tehillim* along with all the other people there. I answered *amen* to Kaddish, and also cried for the boy I had so wanted to meet and would now never meet.

When the memorial service was over and everyone left the grave, I looked back — to see and remember the place.

I also turned around because I wanted to

look at the letter I'd left there, peeking out from under a small stone.

It was the last letter — the one I hadn't been able to give him.

I am positive he knows what I wrote in it, but it was important to me to keep my promise: To give it to him when we met.

Crembo

My name is Yossi and I'm in the fifth grade. I'm considered a pretty good student, no small mischief-maker, and popular.

Ever since I turned three, I've never said "*hamotzi*," never washed my hands for a meal, and I've never said *bircas hamazon*.

No, don't be shocked. I'm a religious kid just like you. You wash your hands and say the blessings for bread, but as for me, well, I just never eat bread.

And not only do I keep away from bread, but even from cookies, crackers, rolls, knishes, kugel, spaghetti and anything else that has even a tiny drop of flour.

I'm not allowed to eat flour, get it? One tiny crumb of flour — and I throw up all the food I've eaten and keep on throwing up for a whole day after that.

I have what's called a "sensitivity to wheat."

I'm not allowed to eat any kind of wheat product. And what's flour made of? Wheat! Now do you understand why I can't eat everything on that long list?

Go ahead and ask me: "Then what can you eat?" The answer: Everything else! Meat, eggs, candy, popcorn, Bamba, fruits and vegetables, dairy products (popsicles, ice-cream...) and I practically forgot — Crembo!

But with Crembo I have a problem. I'm allowed to eat the "Crem" — the white fluffy cream inside — and the chocolate icing, too, but not the "Bo," the cookie part. I can't eat it because it's made of wheat.

When I was little, it was a big problem. I would forget I couldn't eat it and I'd finish the Crembo until the end. Then I would have terrible stomach pains. But as time went on my mother taught me that first I have to separate the "Crem" from the "Bo," and eat just the cream.

And that's what I did.

Over the years all the kids in my class got used to jumping on me every time Crembos were given out. Everyone knew that I couldn't eat the cookie part and they all pleaded, "Yossi, give me yours!" "Yossi, give it to me!" I used to carefully separate the "Bo" from the "Crem" to make sure I wouldn't miss a drop of it (it sticks, in case you didn't know) and then afterwards I would give it to someone. Usually it was someone I hadn't given it to for a long time.

Years passed that way. In the meantime, someone told my mother that it's possible to buy something very similar to flour and to bake bread that tastes exactly like regular bread. Since then, I started to bring delicious rolls to school, and my friends started to be jealous (even though they didn't have anything to be jealous of).

On the other hand, no one had yet found a solution for the cookie part of the Crembo.

One Shabbos, when we finished saying *Te-hillim*, I got a Crembo from the people in charge of the group, as usual. Suddenly, one little boy whom I hardly knew came over to me and gave me...his Crembo.

Before I had a chance to ask him why, he took the Crembo back from me, took off the wrapper, separated the cookie from the cream, made the *mezonos* blessing, put the cookie part into his mouth, and gave me back the "Crem."

"What are you giving it to me for?" I asked him.

"You probably don't remember me," said the boy while chewing the cookie, "but since I was in kindergarten I've gotten about four Crembo cookies from you, and I never gave you anything back. That's why I decided that it was about time that I gave you something, too."

I was shocked. No one had ever acted this way before.

"But I'm not going to eat the cookie part anyway," I told him. "It's not like a kid giving up something he wants to eat."

"True," said the boy, "but it always made me mad to see all the boys pushing and shoving to ask you to give it to them, as if you owed it to them, without even saying thank you. My father told me that if someone does you a favor, you have to appreciate it. And that's what I did."

I liked this kid, believe me.

"What grade are you in?" I asked.

"Second," he answered.

"Thanks a million," I told him. "It's funny that a little kid I don't even know is acting so nice."

"I'm not a little kid," he said. "I'm in second grade — didn't I say that already?"

"Sorry," I said. "I didn't mean to hurt your feelings. You really are big. I would even want to be your friend, okay?"

"Okay," said the boy. "You also look like a nice kid."

We shook hands and parted.

I took a few steps and suddenly realized that I hadn't asked him his name.

"What's your name?" I shouted after him.

He turned around. "I see that you really do want to be my friend," he said. "My name is Yitzi. 'Yitzi-pitsy,' they call me."

"You're not little," I told him. "Did you forget?"

We both laughed and went on our way. And I knew that I had made a new friend, a smart boy with good *middos*. I haven't found a better friend yet.

Look what can happen all because of a Crembo!

The Old Man near the School

My name is Benny. I'm in the fifth grade.

The school I go to is very close to an apartment building. The windows of the building face the windows of the classrooms, and the balconies of the building are right opposite our playground.

On the first floor of the building, practically right on top of us, lives an old man. We didn't know his name. The only thing we knew about him was that he very, very much didn't like us.

Every recess he used to stand on his balcony, shout at the kids, shake his fist and threaten them.

Practically every other day he would go to the principal's office to complain about the "short boy in the blue-striped shirt who was shouting during recess and making a disturbance," or about "the one who makes so much noise kicking the ball."

The principal used to speak with him politely, but would wave away his complaints. He would explain to him each time, in a quiet yet firm manner, that children need to play and kick balls and sometimes even shout. "These are the hours during which they are allowed to play," the principal used to tell him each time. "You have to understand — they're children."

But the old man would shake his fist angrily, shout at the principal, and leave the office, slamming the door and shouting at us as he left. Once, someone acted fresh to him. The principal called the boy over and gave him a big punishment. "Your job is to play, not to be fresh to someone older than you, even if you think he's not right," he said.

And he really wasn't right, that old man, believe me. He was a very difficult person, and I think he was just looking for an excuse to argue.

From the time I was in kindergarten, I remember this old man shouting, threatening and complaining. More than once he called the police. The patrol car used to stop with a screech next to the school, the policemen would go inside angrily to the principal's room — and come out apologetic. They realized the charges were false. There were times when the policemen wanted to arrest the old man because of the false charges, but the principal always asked them to let it go. "Leave him alone, he's only someone who's all alone — it's probably boring for him," the principal used to say with a smile. And the policemen would let it go.

That's the kind of principal I have, a kind and good man, who always tries to understand other people.

Over the years, we all got used to it. The old man practically became part of our school. Every kid who went to the school knew that he had to get used to the admonishments and threats of the old man, used to the patrol cars which arrived once a month and used to the talks with the principal, who acted respectfully towards the old man and didn't try to irritate him. They just got used to it.

One day when we were playing during recess, I noticed that something was different. It didn't take me long to figure out what. It was the old man. He wasn't standing on his balcony looking angry and he wasn't shouting at anyone. It really made a difference.

"It's great," I told my friend Shmulik. "He's probably sleeping late today and decided to give us a little peace and quite."

The same thing happened during the next recess. The old man just never appeared. "He probably went to the doctor's," volunteered Gadi (and Gadi was an expert on doctors, since he spent a lot of time waiting for them...)

"Forget it, what difference does it make?" shouted Shmulik. "Benny, how about playing already? Gadi, maybe you want to go look for him at the doctor's?" fumed Shmulik.

We laughed and began to play.

The next day was the same.

On the third day, at the end of the first break, we headed back for our classrooms. Before I was swallowed up inside the building, I glanced towards the balcony. He wasn't there.

The next day we were also able to play during the morning break without the usual interruptions. I found myself looking all the time towards the balcony above the yard. I can't explain why. Maybe it was sort of a habit to see the old man shouting and shaking his fists at us.

At the lunch break I started to worry. The old man hadn't yelled at us for two days already. I was positive something was wrong.

"Maybe we should go up to his apartment to see what's going on?" I suggested to my friend, Gershon.

"Are you crazy?" he said. "Don't you have

anything better to do? He'll throw you down the stairs."

I kept quiet. He was probably right. The old man wasn't exactly the kindest person in the world, and there was no reason to risk a visit to him.

When recess was over, I went into the classroom feeling very upset. Class began, but I couldn't concentrate. I imagined the old man laying there in bed, only a few yards away from us. Maybe he couldn't move, or was crying for help, and no one...

I raised my hand.

"Yes, Benny," said the teacher.

"Uh, I need to go out," I said.

"To where?" asked the teacher.

"To...to see what's going on with the old man who shouts."

"Excuse me?" said the teacher in astonishment. Twenty-eight pairs of eyes, some of them laughing, turned to me. The teacher called me to follow him outside the classroom. I told him what I was worried about. His expression turned serious, and he said, "Go to Reb Yosef the janitor and tell him what you just told me now."

I did what he said. The janitor took what I said seriously and said to me, "Let's go to his house together."

We went. We went up one flight of stairs. Reb Yosef knocked on the door.

No answer was heard.

"Maybe he went to the doctor's?" said the janitor, reminding me slightly of Gadi...

"For two days?" I asked.

Reb Yosef looked at me and smiled. "You're right," he said. "It is worrisome."

The knocks turned into thunderous pounding. A neighbor from the second floor came out and asked, "Why are you making so much noise?"

We told him that we were worried about the man who lived in the apartment. The neighbor said something vague and closed the door.

"That's neighbors for you," said Reb Yosef and renewed his pounding on the door.

"Let's listen," I said. "Maybe he's calling for help."

Reb Yosef stopped pounding on the door and both of us pressed our ears to it.

A minute of silence passed. We didn't hear a thing except for some rustling sounds which probably came from the street.

Reb Yosef motioned me to keep on listening. "Our ears need to get used to the noise. Maybe then we'll hear something."

Reb Yosef knocked another time. We kept on listening for a while and suddenly my ears picked up a faint moan.

I looked over at Reb Yosef and pointed to my ear. He signaled me that he didn't hear anything. I put my finger on my lips and put my ear back up against the door.

A weak sound was heard from inside, like heavy breathing. "Maybe he can't get up from the bed," I said. "Let's call the fire department."

"There's no time for the fire department," said Reb Yosef. "Move."

I moved from my place. Reb Yosef stepped back from the door and suddenly threw himself at it, kicking it with all his might. A sound of splintering wood was heard. The door moved a little, but stayed locked.

Reb Yosef took a few steps back again. He was a short, thin man. I wouldn't have believed that he had such strength.

I saw an expression of intense concentration and effort on his face. He threw himself again at the door and kicked it with tremendous force. It splintered and was torn off its hinges.

We went into the hall, and as soon as we got to the kitchen we saw him.

He was laying on the floor at the kitchen entrance. He looked awful. His face was white as a sheet. When he saw us he tried to get up, but then his head fell back and his eyes closed.

Reb Yosef yelled to me, "Find a phone and

call an ambulance." He immediately bent over the old man and checked to see if he was breathing.

I rushed to look for a phone. Reb Yosef's expression told me that the old man's condition was not good. I started to look all over the apartment but couldn't find a phone. From the kitchen I heard the sounds of artificial respiration and then Reb Yosef called out to me, "Come back — the phone's here."

I raced back to the kitchen. I saw Reb Yosef pressing his hands on the old man's chest. I punched 101 and whispered, "Come to..." and I gave them the address. "There's an old man here who's not breathing. Hurry."

Reb Yosef stopped what he was doing to check the old man's neck for a pulse. I knew what he was doing. My father is part of Hatzala, and more than once told me how they take care of people in situations like this.

"He has a pulse," I heard Reb Yosef say.

He continued to give him artificial respiration. In the background we heard the wails of the ambulance's siren. They drew closer until it was clear that the ambulance had arrived.

Within a few seconds a few paramedics appeared. They started to treat the old man, gave him a shot, and after a few minutes one of them said, "That's it, we can take him now."

They put the old man on a stretcher and started to take him out. I followed them, but turned when I suddenly heard the sound of a body falling behind me.

It was Reb Yosef. He had fainted from the excitement and strain.

I called out to the paramedics. "Hey, there's someone here who's fainted."

They put the stretcher down, went over to Reb Yosef and stood him on his feet. His eyes opened right away and he said, "Leave me alone, it's only from the tension. Take care of the old man."

After they went down with the stretcher, one of them came right back upstairs and took Reb Yosef to the ambulance.

In the meantime, the principal of the school appeared and asked to come along. So the ambulance went with one patient in the stretcher, one person who had fainted sitting on the side bench, and a principal to watch over both.

Later in the day, Reb Yosef was released. He called me when he got home to tell me about it. I was happy and asked how the old man was.

"He'll pull out of it in a few days," said Reb Yosef. "He's suffering from a broken hip bone, weakness, and malnutrition. If you hadn't gotten to him, he would have died within a couple of minutes."

"How could it be that exactly the minute we got to him he stopped breathing?" I asked.

Reb Yosef answered me, "That's it. God, when He wants someone to live, gives that person super-natural powers. God sent an angel to watch over the old man and then put into the head of a human being the idea to help him. The wonders of Hashem!"

That same day I went with Reb Yosef to visit the old man. He was attached to a lot of machines, but his condition had improved. When he saw me, he got very excited, and there were tears in his eyes. It was hard for him to talk. But after a while, Reb Yosef encouraged him and he began to tell us what had happened to him.

"I went out to the kitchen at night to drink when suddenly I slipped and fell. I tried to get back up but I felt terrible pains in my hip. They were really paralyzing pains.

"I tried to call for help, but no one heard me. I fainted a number of times from the pain and from an overwhelming weakness. Every time I woke up I called for help and tried to crawl towards the telephone. I managed to get close to it, but I just couldn't get up. I stretched out my arm towards the phone, but I couldn't reach it, even though I knew that with its help I could save my life. I lay there discouraged and confused." Again, tears appeared in his eyes, and he found it hard to continue his story.

"My shouts became weaker. I felt terribly hungry. I ate a few crumbs that were on the floor, and suddenly I was sorry that I was such a clean and orderly person, who hardly had any crumbs.... All too soon I realized that I had no chance of staying alive, because I have no relatives or friends. I realized, to my great dismay, that I could lay there forever, until I would die of hunger and suffering. I was afraid...believe me, so afraid.... I prayed to the Creator of the world that He take me fast, so that at least I wouldn't have to suffer.

"Several days passed that way. I couldn't even count how many. I found myself awaiting death, and slowly fell into a deep sleep, on the way to death... And then you came, my rescuers. How did you even think of me?" he asked Reb Yosef.

"I don't even know you," said Reb Yosef. "It's him — the boy," he said and pointed to me. I blushed.

"And how do you know me?" asked the old man.

I hesitated. "I, um, I see you on the balcony above the school yard."

"But how did you notice that I wasn't there? Children don't pay attention to old people, even if they're neighbors."

I didn't say anything.

"Tell me. I'm just curious as to why all of a sudden you thought of me."

I blushed even harder. I was embarrassed to tell him why I had noticed his absence. But he proved himself to be a stubborn person (actually, I always knew him to be that way) and didn't let me get away with not telling him.

I decided to tell him.

"I just noticed that...no one...no one...was shouting at us."

Both of them, Reb Yosef and the old man, burst out laughing. Reb Yosef's laugh was full and healthy, while the old man broke out in a chorus of coughs because of how hard he was laughing.

When he had calmed down, the old man said, "So that's it? My shouts? Who would have believed... It's certainly not a pleasant matter. What can I say? That I'll stop shouting at all of you? What would happen to me the next time I fall? Who would notice?"

I thought about that. He was right, actually. Who would notice an old man who didn't shout and didn't make trouble? Would I have noticed his absence if he had been a quiet person who didn't make any trouble for us?

The visit came to an end. I agreed to the old man's request that I visit him again.

Reb Yosef's "few days" turned into a month. At the end, they released the old man, who by now I knew by name — Mr. Moshe Shenkman — and he went home.

One day after his release I appeared at his house, along with some of my friends from class, with a cake my mother had specially baked. He was excited to see us, but said that he wasn't allowed to eat a cake like that, and immediately cut it into pieces and gave it to us. We wolfed it down.

"Look, about what you asked me," I said. "I have an idea."

"About what?"

"About that, that kids don't pay attention to old people," I said.

He remembered. "Nu, what's your idea?"

"I think that this story will make it clear to kids how much old people need some connection with them, how important it is not to stay away from old people and even to ask how they are and see how they're doing."

"Nu," said the old man, "so what are you going to do?"

"I'll make the story known to all the kids. I think that will help," I said.

"How exactly will you make it known?"

"There's a mail box that kids send their stories to. Don't worry, it'll become known."

The old man looked doubtful, but I knew exactly what I was going to do.

As soon as I got home, I sat down and wrote this long letter, and after that I folded it and put it in an envelope on which I had written:

To: "Kids Speak"
       P.O.B. 211
       Bnei Brak, Israel

Now I'm waiting. I wonder if it will ever get published.

Be My Brother

My name is Meir. I'm in the sixth grade and am a pretty hard-working kid. I get along great with my friends.

I have a huge problem that makes me very sad. I'm positive that anyone reading this will find it hard to believe that my story is true.

I have one brother whose real name I don't want to mention. I'll just call him Yehuda. He is the oldest in our family and he's in the eighth grade.

From the time I was in kindergarten my brother has pestered me and my other brothers and sisters. The situation got worse from day to day. He would hit us, demand that we tell him everything, and if he didn't like something, he would curse and call us names. He really scared everyone, and caused a lot of trouble for the whole family. When my parents saw that he was getting worse, they decided to take him to an expert. The expert did actually manage to help him improve in school work, but right about then my brother decided that I was the cause of all his troubles. He was probably jealous of me because the other kids in the house treated me like the oldest brother since I treated them nicely.

He started to hate me.

It wasn't like some ordinary fight between brothers — it was real hatred. He just decided to pick on me, to beat me up for any little thing, to "confiscate" things that belonged to me, and to bother me in every way possible.

The situation got so bad that one day I burst out crying and said to my parents, "You have a problem with one child, but I feel that soon you'll have a problem with another." I didn't just say it, either. I really felt it. There were moments when I felt that there wasn't any more strength left in me.

After consultations between my parents and my teacher, it was decided that I would live at my uncle's house for a while.

Even though this solution wasn't fair, it was a great solution because suddenly, all at once, all the torment stopped. Sometimes I didn't see my brother for a whole month (because my parents made sure that on a Shabbos when I'd come, he'd be a guest somewhere else).

I know that this story sounds very strange, but that was my fate.

I stayed at my uncle's house for quite a few months until something happened that completely changed everything.

One day, after school, my uncle sent me on an errand. I set off in the direction of the place, which was very close to my old school.

Not far from the entrance to the school I saw a group of boys fighting. I realized my brother was picking a fight with six boys from his class. He was acting wild and kicking in all directions, but they were, of course, stronger than he, because of their numbers. They overpowered him and punched him.

At first, my brother tried to resist with all his might, but he was soon overcome. He lay flat out on the ground and they started to kick him.

I stood there with mixed feelings. On the one hand, I knew that he was to blame and that they were probably punishing him for what he had done to them. On the other hand, I felt a responsibility for him. A small voice inside me whispered that I should get involved.

I went closer.

Blood flowed from my brother's nose, and he was really suffering. His friends spotted me and wanted to see how I'd react. They all knew how great the relationship was between us.

I didn't know what to do, either. Suddenly, I didn't know what pushed me, I ran into the group and said, "Stop it! Don't you think you've gone too far?"

A few of them started to push me aside, saying, "Don't butt in. You know exactly who your brother is." I shook myself loose and went back again to protect my beaten and bruised brother.

During my efforts to protect him, I must've hurt some of them with my hands. They left my brother and started to hit me.

I had never gotten hit that hard before. Within seconds, punches and kicks rained down over every part of my body. At first I tried to resist, but it was obvious that the six of them would overpower me. They threw me down and did exactly what they had done minutes before to my brother.

I sensed that I was badly hurt. Blood flowed from my nose.

I fainted.

When I woke up, they were no longer around. I lay there wounded and beaten in the middle of the yard. I tried to get up, but my hands and feet refused to obey. I felt very weak and was afraid of fainting again.

That instant I heard a sound behind me. I

turned around and saw my brother barely managing to stand on his feet. He got up very slowly. His clothes were torn and blood-stained. He looked at me and I at him.

A lot of thoughts went through my mind during those moments. I felt a strong desire to cry about the situation I was in, and actually, about my whole life.

My brother came over to me and said, "Get up."

"I can't get up," I said.

I saw him hesitate. "Can't you get up by yourself?"

I tried, but I felt a sharp pain in my right hand and my left foot.

When my brother saw how hard I was trying, he come over, squatted down, and held my hand gently. I screamed.

"It's probably broken," he said. He held my other hand, put his hand under my arm and helped me stand on my feet.

My left foot hurt. I almost couldn't step on it. He started to carry me to the street, and I limped after him, our bodies close together. He didn't say anything — he just breathed heavily. The effort was hard for him, especially since he too had gotten a beating.

He brought me to our house, the home I had left months before. The neighbors looked at us

in astonishment. I didn't blame them. It was a surprising scene, especially for anyone who knew about our past relationship.

We got to the elevator. I saw that he wanted to ask me something but couldn't decide. I didn't say a thing. When the elevator came, we got in it. The elevator started to go up, and then he asked, "Meir, why — why did you take my side?"

I looked at him and I wanted to answer, but I didn't know what to answer. I didn't have any answer.

I remembered the difficult times I had been through because of him, and the question he had asked arose in my heart, too. Why?

I saw he was waiting for an answer, and then I just burst out sobbing over the strange things I had to go through in my life.

I knew that the suffering was over. There was an understanding between us, a wordless understanding. I cried over the things that had happened between us, and felt pain that the understanding had come so late. Could we ever be like two regular brothers? I asked myself.

I glanced at him, and for the first time, I saw his lips trembling and his eyes blinking back tears. And then he did what I had never, ever seen him do before. He burst out crying.

With the two of us standing there sobbing,

our arms wrapped around each other, the door of the elevator opened and there was...my mother.

You could see the shock on her face. "Wh-what happened to you? What are you do-ing here?"

My brother took my arm and supported me as we left the elevator. He looked at my mother and in a sobbing voice said to her only three words: "We came home."

Inferiority Complex

My name is Nava and I'm in the sixth grade. In our family there are eight children, *bli ayin hara*. The oldest is sixteen, and I'm the third in the family.

My problem is that I have an inferiority complex.

What's that? That's when a person pities herself, like a girl who thinks she's loved less than everyone else...and maybe not at all. It's when a person thinks that no one pays attention to her or cares about her.

I notice even the smallest little thing and read meaning into it. If, for instance, we're all going to the zoo and my sister is the one to hold all the money, I feel that they're favoring her over me, so I say, "What's the matter — don't you trust me?"

When my father comes to take us in the car, it matters a lot to me if my sister sits up front and not me. You're probably thinking that it's just jealousy, but with me, it's not jealousy but a feeling that people don't respect me, as if I'm not that important in the house.

Sometimes, I get angry over things and afterwards I'm sorry. Once, for instance, my mother told me to run an errand outside the house (in our family, we like helping around the house better than running errands outside it). But then my mother said to my sister, "You'll help me here around the house." Right away, I felt that my mother was keeping her at home and sending me because she loved her more. I said it out loud, and then my sister said, "Great, then I'll go. Bye!" and left me at home.

I was furious with myself and with my sister. My mother, who saw that I was still upset, asked me, "Why are you angry now? Look, she gave in to you and you're here with me." I didn't have any answer, so I said, "You both planned the whole thing so that I'd want to stay here."

I guess you've gotten the idea of what "inferiority complex" means.

What's interesting is that deep down in my heart I know that my feelings aren't right and that I'm just insecure, because it can't be that they like me less.

The problem is, I've never had any proof. I guess kids who are insecure need constant reassurance and proof that they're loved.

One time, during Pesach vacation, we went to Nachal David. I noticed that along the way there were a lot of Bedouin tents. My father talked the whole way about the places we passed, that is, he was like a tour guide. Suddenly I said to him, "Right you're talking and telling us all this to distract us, so that we'll forget about the tents and won't be afraid?"

Daddy and Mommy burst out laughing, which showed everyone that I was right. My mother hugged me and murmured to my father in Yiddish (so that I wouldn't understand), "There's nothing to do about it, this girl is just smart."

You don't know how happy I was when I heard that. All of a sudden I had proof that my mother loved and admired me. I just need reassurance. If an inferiority complex is a disease, then compliments and reassurance are its cure.

I think that my mother also sensed my happiness, and from then on she tried to compliment me and tell me again how much she loves me. That reassures me a lot.

But this week, in the middle of summer vacation, something happened that taught me a lot about my feelings of insecurity.

I made up with my friend Batsheva to meet at three o'clock on Shabbos afternoon. Batsheva is one of the best friends I have left (I quarreled with a lot of the others because I thought they didn't want to be friends with me, or because I suspected them of talking about me behind my back).

I got to the place we agreed on at 2:55 and waited patiently.

Five minutes passed, ten minutes, twenty minutes. I waited until 3:45, and when I saw that Batsheva wasn't coming, I went home mad and hurt.

I didn't tell my mother a thing. I was embarrassed to tell her that my friend had avoided me like that. In my heart, though, I thought, How could Batsheva do something like that to me? How could she make me leave home on Shabbos when the sun was blazing and let me stand there waiting? I realized that she must have made up to meet another friend and was too ashamed to tell me.

I felt like my whole vacation was ruined. I was very tense. Inside, I was furious and very hurt about what Batsheva had done to me on Shabbos. I kept on asking myself, Why did she avoid meeting me? Besides that, I asked myself who was left for me to be friends with. These thoughts brought on another pain — I had quarreled with too many friends.

My parents saw that I was in a terrible mood. I didn't want to go anywhere, even though vacation was almost over. They didn't say a thing to me, though. They were used to my moods.

Monday night, when I was deep in my sad thoughts, my little brother asked me to tell him a story. I told him that I didn't feel like it. He asked again and again and I lashed out at him suddenly with horrible shouts, as if someone had bitten me.

My brother was shocked into silence, and everyone looked at me in horror. I started to cry.

My mother put the kids to sleep, and later in the evening when my father came home he was told that "there's a problem with Nava." He told me to sit down at the table and then asked what happened.

There was no point in refusing to answer. He would have gotten out of me what was bothering me anyway. That's how my father is.

I told my parents about what had happened on Shabbos and about how angry I was with Batsheva.

When I finished my story and complained that I didn't have any friends and that they all dropped me, my father smiled and said, "I want you to call Batsheva right away. I am one hundred percent certain that she had a reason for not coming."

I refused. "*I* should call *her?* After what she did to me? Never!"

But my father was positive he was right. "I know her," he said. "You like to make everything come out looking bad. I don't feel what you feel, and I'm telling you that she must have fallen asleep or something like that. I am certain that she didn't do it on purpose."

My father insisted and urged me, and in the end looked through the phone book, wrote down the telephone number and started to dial. He told me, "If you won't talk, I will. It would be a shame for you to be embarrassed."

He listened for several seconds and suddenly put the receiver into my hand. "Talk," he said.

"Hello," a voice was heard.

"Who's speaking?" I asked.

"Rivki." (Rivki was Batsheva's sister.)

"Um, could I please speak with Batsheva?"

"Who is this?"

"Nava."

"Nava? Don't you know that Batsheva is in the hospital?"

"What happened?" I was shocked.

"Friday night she got a very high fever and

fainted. Daddy drove her to the hospital. She has a very dangerous infection. She's unconscious."

I hung up, but not before asking where she was hospitalized and in what room.

I looked at my parents. A smile of victory was spread across my father's face. From my conversation they understood what had happened. It was no time to say "I told you so." A thousand voices in my mind said it for them.

Batsheva regained consciousness yesterday. I was in her room when she woke up. I'm there practically every day. I managed to talk to her. She's too weak to talk, so I'm the one who does the talking. I told her a lot of things, but not what you think. I didn't dare. Not yet.

I think that boys or girls who suffer from an inferiority complex definitely understand what needs to be understood from my story.

Will this story make me more realistic? Less insecure?

I sure hope so!

Study Partners

My name is Avi and I live in Jerusalem. I'm in the eighth grade.

There are thirty students in my class. We study Gemara at a pretty high level. My father says that when he was in *yeshivah ketanah* they learned at this level.

Naturally, studying is not simple. It's not enough to listen to the teacher. To succeed and really master the Gemara and the commentaries you have to prepare the Gemara before class and review it afterwards.

It's hard to prepare it by yourself. Boys who study Gemara know why. Girls, who don't study Gemara, don't always know why it's so hard to understand a page filled with questions and explanations.

I'll try to explain. Let's start with the fact that in the Gemara there is no punctuation, and there are no vowels. There are no question marks or exclamation marks, and it's not always written which *Tanna* made the comments. That means that you have to figure out where the question ends, where the explanation begins, and who said what!

A lot of the words and expressions in the Gemara are written in Aramaic, but it's a language that's not that hard to learn. Mostly what's hard is getting deeply into the *sugya*. Sometimes there's a question and an explanation given for it, and then right after that the Gemara brings a "*stirah*" (contradiction) to that explanation from another Gemara (that is, in a different Gemara the same *Tanna* says exactly the opposite). Then an *Amora* shows that there's a "*chiluk*" (a difference) between that Gemara and ours, which explains the difficulty; but then a different *Amora* attacks this line of reasoning and says that you can't say that because in a third Gemara it's written...

I think I've explained enough about what's hard about studying Gemara. (And I still didn't mention the various other commentators like Rashi, *Tosafos, Rishonim,* and *Acharonim.*)

I must admit that because of all these difficulties the satisfaction you get when you understand the Gemara is very great. That's the second reason yeshivah students use every minute to study. The first is that it's a mitzvah.

When I started to study Gemara, I didn't feel any pleasure in it — only difficulty. The bigger I get, the more I feel satisfaction in learning. But, I must point out, it's still hard for me.

To overcome the difficulty in preparing the Gemara and reviewing it, students usually study *"b'chavruta"* — with a study partner. This is because when two learn together, one can always help the other to understand.

Naturally, every one looks for the most successful and talented study partner. That way there's more of a chance of understanding the Gemara better.

Now, after that long introduction, I'll get to the story.

Chaim'ke is the best student in our class. There's no question that he's the study partner most in demand. Every kid wants to learn with him. That's the reason I called him at the beginning of the year to get him for a study partner.

"Chaim'ke, can I learn with you on Shabbos from twelve o'clock until two in the afternoon?" I asked him over the phone. There was silence on the other side of the line.

"Did you make up with someone else already?" I asked.

"No...but..."

"Don't you want to learn with me?" I asked.

Chaim'ke was silent. The silence became unpleasant.

Finally, Chaim'ke answered hesitantly, "Okay, fine. We'll learn in the Gra shul."

"Thanks," I answered happily and clicked off the phone.

From ten o'clock on Shabbos morning the Gemara was ready on the table, and next to it, my notebook with summaries. I thought happily that if I succeeded this Shabbos in arranging with Chaim'ke to be my regular study partner, I would be able to make great progress in learning. I placed a lot of hopes in this partnership.

At 11:30, I left the house. From my house to the Gra shul was a long, tiring half-hour walk. "Well," I thought, "Torah is acquired through suffering."

I got there at exactly 12:00. I went in. The shul was empty.

I knew that Chaim'ke was very exact about time, so I couldn't understand how it could happen that he wouldn't be there.

I decided to wait for him for a quarter of an hour. After all, he's not an angel. Maybe he had gotten held up.

The minutes crawled by. Five minutes, ten, quarter of an hour — and no sign of Chaim'ke.

I decided to go to his house, thinking that

maybe he was there. I knocked on the door re-
peatedly. His mother opened it.

"*Shabbat shalom*," I said. "Chaim'ke arranged to learn with me in the Gra shul but he
didn't come. Do you know where he is?"

"No," was the answer. "I know that he went
to learn, but I don't know to which shul he
went," said his mother.

I left his house tired and disappointed. But I
still didn't give up. I found myself going from
shul to shul. The sun dried me out completely.
My legs felt weak, but I still didn't give up.

Suddenly I heard a faint sound of voices
coming from inside the Pnei Shemuel shul.
The closer I got to the shul, the stronger the
voices sounded. It sounded like voices learning.

And then I heard the clear voice of
Chaim'ke. I walked quickly over to the shul's
entrance and there, right in front of my eyes, I
saw Chaim'ke studying with Yehuda and
Nachum, fellow classmates....

Nachum, who sat opposite the door and
studied with Chaim'ke, was the first to spot me.
I saw him whisper something hurriedly to
Chaim'ke and Yehuda. They turned around fast
and I saw confusion in their faces. Suddenly
Nachum got up and locked the door of the shul
in my face.

I stood for a minute shocked by the blow.

Why? Why did he do that to me? What did I ever do to him?

Other thoughts hit me like lightning. Chaim'ke, the smartest boy in the class, doesn't want to study with me. So much so, that he went to the trouble of going to a different shul so that I wouldn't meet him.

The agony made me act without thinking.

I started to pull on the door and tried to open it by force. Naturally, I didn't succeed. I leaned helplessly on the stair railing and cried inwardly. "Hashem," I thought. "You, Who knows everyone's thoughts, know how much I want to study Your holy Torah. Please, don't humiliate me."

An elderly man was walking towards the shul. My friends, who saw him, rushed to open the door for him. When I saw that, I realized that Hashem helped me so that I could study with them. I jumped up and managed to get in.

"Okay," said Yehuda, defeated. "We'll let him learn with us this time."

"Okay," they all agreed, and my heart leapt with joy.

We started to study — all four of us. I swallowed my anger and humiliation and threw myself into the Gemara.

After half an hour of learning, which was half an hour of pure pleasure, I noticed the three of them whispering. Suddenly Nachum stood up and declared, "That's it. I have to go home."

"Me too," said Yehuda.

"Me too," announced Chaim'ke.

But this time I wasn't so naive. My first experience had shown me that not everything they said was true. I decided to check it out. I pretended to go home and hid in the bushes. When my friends saw that I had disappeared, they changed their minds and turned to...the Gra shul.

I left my hiding place and went step by step to the Gra shul. From afar, I heard the happy voices of my friends.

"We fixed him," cried Yehuda.

"Yeah," said Nachum. "Let him stop tagging along after us."

I was deeply hurt. "Why aren't they afraid to act that way?" I wondered. I consoled myself with the thought that Chaim'ke hadn't said a word. You could see that he wasn't happy with the whole thing, but that it wasn't easy for him to say anything to them (or maybe I just wanted to think so?).

I went closer to my friends who were enjoying themselves at my expense. "But I want to learn! Why do you want to keep me from learning?" I called out to them.

They turned around in surprise. "Where did you come from?" asked Yehuda with a sneer. "Did you decide to stick to us like glue?"

"Maybe you want to stop tagging along?" added Nachum. "Can't you take a hint?"

No one had ever humiliated me as much. I swallowed the shame silently and followed them into the shul. We sat and studied for another hour, and then we went home — this time for real.

I walked the long way back. When I got home, I opened the door gently, so as not to wake up my parents from their Shabbos nap. I went to my room quickly, and there I put my face in my pillow and started to cry.

"Why do I deserve this?" I wondered. "I really want to learn and grow in Torah. Don't I have a chance? Do I have to keep chasing after the others and humiliating myself?"

For the first time in my life I really understood what "*chavruta* or *metuta* — either a study partner or death" meant.

Wordlessly, I pleaded with Hashem to help me study His holy Torah. I asked Him to open the hearts of my friends.

I thought of a prayer that expressed my request. I found the right verse: "*Avinu, Av haRachaman*...have mercy on us and instill in our hearts understanding, the ability to explain, to hear, to study, to teach, to do and to observe..." and that's how I fell asleep, crying.

A week passed. I didn't talk to Chaim'ke the whole week. I was embarrassed in front of him, and also mad at him. I had already given up on learning with him. I didn't think I had a chance after what happened.

Friday afternoon came. The telephone rang. It was Chaim'ke. "Avi," he said, "I would like to be study partners with you every Shabbos. With you, along with Nachum and Yehuda. Do you agree?"

I felt my heart bursting with happiness. "Sure," I answered. "Thank you."

Chaim'ke hemmed and hawed. He wanted to say something more, but decided against it.

"Come tomorrow as usual at twelve o'clock," he said. "And I'm very sor—"

"That's okay," I interrupted him. "What was, was."

Since then we've been studying together regularly for half a year. Slowly but surely the deep hurt they gave me that Shabbos has healed. At first, I couldn't understand the meaning of the sudden about face in the way they treated me. As time went by, I heard more and more details of what happened that same Shabbos, after I left them.

After they left (they told me), an argument

started between Chaim'ke, and Yehuda and Nachum. Yehuda and Nachum really got it from Chaim'ke for the way they had dragged him into hurting a friend. They refused to take all the blame, though. "Why did you agree to it?" they accused. Chaim'ke admitted that he had also been to blame, but declared, "Either you agree to include him, or I'll learn with him by myself." They had no choice but to agree.

But deep in my heart I know full well the real reason for the change.

It was my prayer, said from the depths of my heart, and the tears: "*Avinu, Av haRachaman*...have mercy on us and instill in our hearts understanding, the ability to explain, to hear, to study, to teach, to do and to observe..."

Adopted

I don't want to say my real name.

I'm ten, and I live somewhere in the southern part of the country.

I'm adopted. I came to my parents at the age of five years old.

When I started going to school, I innocently told my friends that I was adopted. They didn't know exactly what the word meant so I offered to explain it to them. I didn't think there was any reason not to tell.

I told them that my real parents couldn't continue to raise me. I said that I wasn't mad at them for giving me to a different family, because it was for my own good. They loved me and wanted me to have a good life and get a good education. Really, I've got everything they wanted for me. I'm very proud of my new parents and I love them.

At first, none of my friends made a big deal

out of my story. But when I got to the third grade, the kids started to be more and more interested in the story of my adoption. They wanted to know details of how my real parents looked, what they did for a living, and what I thought about them.

Their interest made me start thinking more seriously about the fact that I was adopted. Until then, I accepted my situation and even felt good about it. In conversations with other kids I still wasn't embarrassed to tell them and answer all kinds of questions they asked me out of curiosity. But little by little, I started to feel hurt by it.

Once a friend asked me to show him some pictures from the time I lived with my birth parents.

I didn't do it.

I didn't tell him the reason, but I'm willing to tell you: I'm not wearing a *kippa* and tzitzis in those pictures. I was afraid that the other kids wouldn't understand and would make fun of me.

I started to ask myself a lot of questions because of how the other kids treated me. I didn't have answers for all of them.

For instance, when I would get new things, they used to say to me out of envy, "Because you're adopted, you get everything."

I asked myself, "Don't they get the same things? Does an adopted child get more things from his parents than any other kid? And if so, then why?"

When I thought about it, I felt that they didn't understand that it was sometimes hard for me to get used to the fact that I was separated from my parents, and that they were living with their parents.

I wonder why so many kids are jealous over nothing. Is there anything to envy about me being adopted?

Why do kids (and big people too, come to think of it) think that the other person is better off? How come they don't know how to appreciate all the good they have?

One day, at the end of a game where my team beat another team of kids from my class, a fight started between us and them. All of a sudden one of the kids started shouting and embarrassing me by calling out, "You're just adopted!"

The rest of the team joined in.

I was shocked. I couldn't understand how they dared to use a matter so personal and private against me and to shout it out loud, as if I had done something wrong.

At first, I stood there rooted to the spot. I couldn't move, I was so shocked. I couldn't

believe that they were doing that to me. But they did.

I ran home crying. My whole body was shaking from crying. I was very hurt.

I got home, went straight to my room and threw myself on the bed, sobbing bitterly. I cried for a long time, until the tears finally stopped and I started to think about what had happened.

From the way the kids yelled, you could tell that it was supposed to be embarrassing to be adopted. I had never thought so before. After all, had I done anything wrong? Had my birth parents or my adoptive parents done anything wrong? All it was, was a soul looking for a place to be raised and educated, and those who had brought this soul into the world had decided that it was best for it not to be raised by them, but by different parents. Did anyone here act in a wrong way?

My mother suddenly came into the room and saw me crying. She quickly tried to find out what had happened to me. At first, I didn't want to tell her, because all of a sudden, I felt embarrassed. It's hard to write this, but those mean kids had made me feel a little, well, distant from my mother. Maybe you won't understand why, but that's how someone feels when he is reminded that his mother is not the one who gave birth to him. Until that moment I hadn't even thought about that fact.

My mother didn't know how to react. In the beginning, she just started to cry. After that, she called all kinds of experts to ask them what she should do. I saw she was tense. I heard her whispering into the phone and sobbing. During those moments I felt very angry at those who had made all this trouble for us and were upsetting my whole family. After all, hadn't I gone through enough upheavals in my life?

I went over to my mother, looked her in the eyes and said to her, "It's enough already! I don't think we should make a big deal over it. You look a little scared. I think you need to calm me down. The way you're acting is scaring me."

She looked at me in astonishment, and said, "You could be a guidance counselor. No one has calmed me down as much as you have right now."

After that she said she was sorry but that she had been a little hysterical. She sat and tried to explain to me that children are not "mean," but just thoughtless. "A child who does not think, will say in a moment of anger whatever he knows, just to irritate and annoy."

I didn't answer. I thought it wasn't fair. I felt

that there was a certain injustice in that they could find a sensitive spot in me to hurt me, but not in others.

My mother, as if reading my thoughts, said, "If you'll think about it deeply, you'll see that it is possible to find some kind of vulnerable point, where he can be hurt, in practically every child. One child is not that thin, the other is not that tall, a third is too tall, the fourth is lazy, and the fifth doesn't know how to run. My son, thank God, has no problems like these, so they discovered he's adopted and decided to use that against him. Why do you think it's something to be ashamed of? Tomorrow they'll say that you're a 'human being.' Will you also be ashamed of that? It's the truth!"

I remained silent. What my mother said made sense. I really am adopted. Why should I think that it's something to be ashamed of? Just because some kid shouted at me, "You're adopted"? And if he would have shouted, "You're a human being," would I have also been hurt?

But really, I continued to think, there's a difference. And then I understood everything.

When a kid wants to hurt someone's feelings, he always finds the thing that makes the other kid different from everyone else. For instance, against Avi, they discovered that he was "fat"; against Yisrael, that he was "skinny"; against Eli, that he was "short"; and against me, that I'm "adopted."

That means that I'm not different from the others. Because each and every one has a certain difference, and this is just what they found to say against me.

That made me feel a lot better. The word "adopted" suddenly took on a much less scary meaning.

But there's one question left without any answer.

Why do kids hurt each other?

Yair, Come Home

My name is Rafi. I live in Jerusalem and I'm in the sixth grade.

My family is an ordinary family. I have four brothers and three sisters. Three of my brothers are already in yeshivah, one sister is in high school, and the other two are in elementary school.

My father studies Torah all day, and he is called an "*avreich chashuv*." My father really cares about our education. He finds out from us what we're studying, tests our knowledge and is in constant contact with our teachers.

What I want to tell about began a year and a half ago. It's something that is very hard for me to write about. It causes a lot of pain to me and my family.

It's about my brother, Yair.

He is sixteen years old and has already been in a few yeshivos. I'll tell you a secret: Right now, he's not studying anywhere.

From what I hear around the house, it all started because of friends who were a bad influence. At first, we didn't notice anything, but as time went by, even I saw how Yair, who had always been a wonderful boy with a good heart, changed, how he walked around bitter, acted fresh to my father and mother, and sometimes disappeared from the house to go off with his bad friends.

All of a sudden, Yair started having fights with my brothers and sisters. My brothers shouted at him that he was embarrassing them, and my sister in the eighth grade once shouted at him angrily, "Because of you, I won't get accepted into any high school!" Yair looked at her with a hard-to-read expression, and she burst out crying.

I was also pretty embarrassed by him. My friends always have all kinds of bad things to say about him. They don't understand that it hurts my feelings and embarrasses me.

For a long time I kept this pain inside. I used to walk down the street and think that everyone was pointing at me and saying, "There's the one whose brother is a bum." This pain preoccupied me and disturbed my studies, and even made me withdraw within myself.

I never talked about it with my parents. I

just used to listen to their conversations. Actually, my father practically stopped being interested in us. Every spare minute of his time was devoted to Yair. He tried to arrange various places for him to go to school, and arranged for important people to talk to him. Once I told him that because of all the concern over Yair he was forgetting about me a little, but the minute I said it, I was sorry. My father looked at me with such pain that I felt as if he had aged a few years all at once.

He didn't know what to answer me, and only said, "Rafi, if you only knew, you would understand," and didn't say anything more.

During that time I felt a kind of fury towards my brother. Sometimes when he came home I wanted to shout at him, "Look what you're doing to Abba and Imma! Look how you're destroying your family! Don't you care?" But I only said that in my imagination, because I didn't dare say that to Yair to his face, and also because everyone else said exactly the same thing and it didn't help. So how could I, his kid brother, have any influence on him?

Unlike the way he acted towards my older brothers and sisters, whom Yair treated with disdain and hatred, he treated me and my little sister great.

He was willing to sit with us and play for

hours. He was the one who taught me and my sister chess. It wasn't easy. He had to patiently teach us all the rules and all the tricks. During these times he would go back to being the same Yair he used to be, before he went down-hill. He didn't act like a chutzpadik bully, but like a sensitive, good teenager. I never under-stood this contrast in his personality.

Once, after a fierce argument with my mother, he sat down to play with us. I really didn't want to play with him, because he had acted disrespectfully towards Imma and had actually made her cry. I saw that he was still upset, but when he was around us, he kept calm, as if he wanted to pretend to us that nothing had happened. But we saw all too well what had happened. We started to play with him, when all of a sudden Imma came and shouted at him, "I don't want you to play with them! I don't want you to ruin them too! It's enough that one of my children has been de-stroyed. I don't want you to play with him, do you hear? Leave my children alone, don't ruin them! Do you understand? Get out of our lives...."

Yair turned chalk white. Without so much as a glance at me and my sister, he got up and left.

Yair didn't come home. My parents were

very worried that day, even though it wasn't
the first time he had disappeared. I saw pain
and hopelessness on my parents' faces. Loath-
ing for Yair entered my heart. How could he do
that to his parents, to his family?

I took refuge in my room and thought about
the whole thing. I was sad and depressed. What
troubles we have, I thought, and I can't even do
anything to help.

From the hallway I heard my mother telling
my father what had happened. He told her that
she shouldn't have humiliated Yair in front of
the younger children. "They may very well be
his only connection to the family," he said. "He
is going through a difficult period. We must not
cut him off completely."

My parents continued their conversation,
and I decided to think about what my father
had said, that Yair was "going through a
difficult period," and, "they may very well be
his only connection to the family." I, Rafi, and
my sister, Shevi, were Yair's only link to the
family. I thought about that. There was
something to it. We were the only ones who
were still on good terms with him — not
because we weren't angry at him, but because
we didn't dare say to him what others did say
to him. I started to think about the conflict in
Yair's personality. On the one hand, he was a

bum and a chutzpadik kid who didn't care about anything. It didn't even bother him to make his parents mad or to hurt them. On the other hand, I thought about Yair the sensitive and considerate brother, the one who played with us, who gave in to us, who never, ever got angry at us. Yair the complimentary and the patient. How could it be, I wondered. Who is the real Yair? Maybe these were the results of the "difficult period" he was going through?

Suddenly I knew what Yair was missing. The solution appeared before my eyes. How could I not have seen it all along? I knew that now I had an important mission. I didn't know how I would put it into action, and I was also afraid. But the suffering expressions on my parents' faces stayed in my mind and I decided to act.

First of all, I had to find Yair. I decided to try to remember the telephone conversations he had when we played chess. One name kept coming up over and over again in those conversations. I realized that it must be the name of one of those same friends we had so much wanted him to stay away from.

I flipped through the phone book. I looked for that friend's last name. There were about twenty names like it. I decided to call and ask for David (the name of the friend).

On the first call, they answered that they did have that last name, but said that "there's no David here." The same for the second and third. Only on the fourth call did they say that there was a "David," but that he wasn't home. When I asked where he was, I heard the woman (his mother?) sigh and say, "I wish I knew." She gave the name of another family and their phone number, where I might be able to find him.

I called. A boy who wasn't happy to cooperate with me answered the phone. At first he said, "He's not here" — and hung up. I called again and said to him that it was very urgent. His voice turned suspicious. I decided to use all my charms of persuasion. "My name is Rafi. You know my brother, Yair?"

He answered in the affirmative.

"I have to reach him. I'm only in the sixth grade, and I have to meet him today. Do me a favor, I'm begging you," I said.

The boy softened. "Okay, okay, I'll try to find out where David is. He probably knows where Yair is. Call in another quarter of an hour."

I nervously counted fifteen minutes and dialed the number.

The boy answered again. "You're a stubborn kid," he said, and gave me the phone number of a certain bakery where David worked.

I tried calling. No one answered. I decided to go there.

I went out into the hallway. My father and mother were sitting in the next room talking.

"Can I go?" I asked.

"To where?" they both asked.

"To, uh, to...someplace."

My parents reacted with suspicion. I understood them. After what they went through with Yair...

I decided that I should tell them. "I'm going to meet with Yair," I said.

"With Yair? What for? How do you know where he is?" the questions rained down. My parents looked very upset.

"Abba, you said before that me and Shevi are maybe Yair's only link to the family. I want to say something to Yair that will make him come back. That's all."

"What will you say to him?" my father asked.

I didn't say anything. I hadn't prepared anything to say to Yair. I knew that I was going to say what I felt in my heart towards him. I didn't know what words I would use, and anyway, I couldn't say it to my parents. I didn't even know how I'd manage to say what I thought of saying to Yair himself. But what urged me on was the strong desire to have everything work out.

"It's very hard for me to tell you what I plan on saying to Yair," I told my parents, and before they had a chance to answer, I took a deep breath and said, "I can tell you what I don't plan to say. I'm not going to tell him that he's really embarrassing me and the whole family. I'm not going to say to him that he's acting like a bum, that he's killing his parents. I'm not going to say to him that because of him his sister won't be accepted into any high school, and I won't say to him that because of him my friends tease me sometimes. I'm not going to go and say all those things to him because he already knows it all by heart. Will you let me go, Abba, to tell him some different things?"

My father suddenly gave me a look I had never seen before. I saw his face light up. He said, "I never heard anything as clever as what you just said. I understand what you're saying. I guess I know what you're planning on saying. Go ahead, Rafi, tell him what you feel in your heart. I trust you, you are clever and wise. Good luck, and see you later."

Before I left, he called me over to him and kissed me on the cheek. "Pass that on to him, too," he said.

I left for the bakery. I ran as fast as I could. I

got there within twenty minutes.

I asked for David. They didn't know who I was talking about, and then I used the nickname Yair used to call David.

"Ah, Dutzu?" they answered. "He's in the office."

I went up to the office. "Where's Dutzu?" I asked. One man pointed his finger at a youth about Yair's age who sat with his back to me.

I went over to him and introduced myself.

"You're Rafi?" he said. "Yair talks about you a lot."

"I need to speak to him."

"Yair is very hurt. He doesn't want to talk with anyone from his family."

"Where is he?"

"He made me promise not to say."

"You have to tell me where he is," I repeated.

"I have to *not* tell you where he is. I've known him for a long time. He's my friend. You, I don't know, except for the stories he's told me about you."

I felt dizzy, as if I was caught in a maze. I couldn't find the right words. And then I had an idea.

"Listen. I'm positive that you know how to get in touch with him. I'm going down now to the park, and I'm going to wait there until he comes, even if it takes a week. Tell him that.

Tell him I have to talk to him." That's what I said, and I started going downstairs.

"He's not going to come. He's not even in town," Dutzu shouted after me.

"I'm waiting until he comes. I'm positive that he can get here within a week from any-place in the country," I said.

It was six o'clock. It was during the summer, and the sun still hadn't set. I sat in the park, watching the boys and girls playing, but mostly I waited.

7:00. Still light. I went to *daven* Mincha in the shul nearby.

7:30. Ma'ariv. When it was over, the park was empty. The children had all gone home.

8:00. I looked at my watch and couldn't be-lieve that I'd already been waiting for two hours. I went over to the pay phone to let my parents know that everything was all right and that I was waiting for Yair.

9:00. It was dark. The stores were starting to close up, and I knew that I wouldn't be able to wait much longer.

Even though I had said "a week," that was only to make Dutzu, if he cared about me at all, pass on the message to Yair.

9:15. Yair appeared.

"You're crazy," he said. "I came specially from Bnei Brak for you. At first, I thought

you'd give up and leave, but Dutzu called me
every half hour and told me that my brother
was still waiting in the park. He called five
times since 6:00. At eight-thirty I got on the
bus. Believe me, just to teach you a lesson I
would have left you here a week."

"You wouldn't have left me here," I said.

"That's what you think," he said.

"It's a fact," I said.

"It just turned out that way," he said.

"It didn't just turn out that way. I just happen to know you," I said.

"Know me? How do you come to know me?
What do you know about me except that you
have to watch out that I don't ruin you." He
spoke in that cynical, bitter voice, that he'd
been using for quite some time.

I felt a lump forming in my throat. "Listen,
Yair. Let me say something to you, okay?" I
talked fast. "I stayed here because I was
positive you would come. I think that I know a
side of you not everyone knows. You show
everyone else a different side. I don't know
why, and I'm also not asking, but me and
Shevi know your good side. Yair, we think that
you have a good heart. The best in the world.
You treat us better than any of our brothers
and sisters. You're patient and you're
considerate, and you have a good soul. No, don't

stop me. Let me talk. I know that there are problems with you. I don't want to go into that, that's not my business. But you can count on it that everyone loves you. You hear only the bad things. I want you to hear the good things, too. I think that because you hear bad things all the time, you get excited and move even further away. I want you to know that people know a lot of good things about you. I want you to know that everyone in the house loves you and we aren't willing to give you up. You have to understand Abba. He's so worried. And me and Shevi can't go on without you and we love you so much. Why am I crying? It's because for the first time I'm telling you everything I feel about you and all the pain inside me is coming out along with it. I know you understand. No, you don't have to cry. I'm not crying out of sadness, but because of all my feelings. You have to come back home. You have to compromise with Abba and Imma, and do what they say, but that's not the problem, right? I saw how much you're willing to give up for someone else. Throughout my whole life, you've always helped me, and once you even got hit because you wanted to protect me. You have no problem with sacrificing for another person. You only want for them to love you the same as everyone, for them to accept you and appreciate you. I'm telling you the truth, that they already love you and appreciate you. Come back, Yair, come back home. I promise you that they'll treat you well...."

I talked and cried, cried and talked, until I fell silent because I didn't have anything else to say.

Silence fell upon us. Yair was withdrawn. He looked confused and upset. "Rafi you're talking like an adult, but you're not an adult. There are things you don't understand. I wish everyone would think about me what you and Shevi think. It would solve all my problems." He fell silent again.

Right then my parents appeared. They looked worried. They knew where I was, because I had told them on the phone when I was waiting. "We were worried about you," they said and didn't continue. You could see that they didn't know what to say to Yair.

I decided to make the most of that moment. "Maybe you'll tell Abba and Imma what I'm too young to understand? Go ahead and talk, take down the walls that surround you, tell them the truth, that you love them and want to listen to them. After that, everything will be easy. Isn't it true?"

Yair nodded his head sheepishly. It was a rare moment in which he was willing to open up and at long last say openly everything in his heart, without the barbs and cynicism that characterized his relationship with our parents for the last year and a half.

"I'm going home to sleep," I said. "Stay here and talk. I'll go home by myself." My father gave me money for the bus, and I went to the bus stop. Before I got on the bus, I glanced back at the park and saw my parents talking easily with Yair. I didn't hear what they said, but I knew that this time something would come out of the conversation.

I don't know what they said during that conversation in the park. What I do know is that my father came over to me for the first and only time, the day afterwards, and told me, "I have learned from all my students — but from my son, most of all."

Yair came back home that very same night. And since then, he's never left — forever.

The Nursery School Teacher

My name is Yisrael, but everyone calls me Srulik. I live in Petach Tikvah and I'm in the fifth grade.

In my neighborhood, there's a nursery school teacher with years of experience who's called Ruthi. Her nursery school has been in existence for twenty years. Even my older brother Benny, who's already married, went to her nursery school. Naturally, I went too.

I don't remember too much from nursery school, but I do remember quite clearly that Ruthi was a great teacher, and seeing her face reminds me that I had a good time in her nursery school.

Ruthi's nursery school was always bursting with children all through the years. In order to get accepted there, you needed a lot of pull, because everyone wanted to register there.

But this year the situation changed. It was all because of one of the mothers, who sent her son and wasn't satisfied. My mother says that out of hundreds of children there will always be someone who isn't satisfied and that's not so terrible. The problem was that this same mother was a big talker and she went to all the mothers in the neighborhood and told them that they shouldn't dare send their children to Ruthi's nursery school because she was very bad and she didn't have any patience with children. This was, of course, a lie, but that mother wanted to hurt Ruthi.

And she succeeded. Most of the mothers decided not to sign up their kids for the nursery school.

Soon enough the word got out in our neighborhood. Everyone knew that Ruthi's nursery school would close next year because no one wanted to go to it.

Everyone, that is, except for Ruthi. No one dared tell her what they were saying about her behind her back, and she had no idea what was in store for her.

My mother was very sorry when she heard about it. She said that it was nothing less than criminal that there were people who blindly follow every lie they're told, like sheep with their eyes closed. Imma said that Ruthi was the best nursery school teacher in the country and that she was sorry that she didn't have a younger child so that she could send him to Ruthi's nursery school.

Imma said all these things in our house, and the whole time I thought that someone should go tell Ruthi what they were planning against her. But I was too embarrassed.

The school year was about to end when one day Ruthi came to visit our house. She sat down in the living room and talked with my mother, and I sat outside and listened to what they were saying.

Ruthi talked with my mother about various things and suddenly said, "Do you know something, Rivi?" (That's my mother's name.) "I don't understand what's going on here. Soon registration for next year will begin, yet no one has yet signed up her child for my nursery school. In the end, they'll all come at the last minute and there won't be room for everyone."

My mother kept quiet and didn't say a thing.

"Go figure people out," said Ruthi. "They're so busy with their own affairs that they forget about the children."

My mother still didn't say anything. I stood there like a statue, and after that my mother said, "Maybe you should ask a few of the mothers to sign up before it's too late?"

I didn't hear Ruthi's answer. She murmured something and then changed the subject.

My mother and Ruthi talked for a few more minutes and then said a friendly good-bye.

After Ruthi left, I went into the room and saw that my mother's mood was gloomy.

"Imma, why didn't you tell her that no one was planning on sending children to her?" I asked.

"It's something you can't understand," my mother told me. "It takes a lot of courage to tell such bad news to a woman."

"But it could save her," I said.

"The suggestion that just might save her, I did tell her," Imma answered. "I didn't have the courage to tell her the truth. I'm not that brave, Srulik," she said.

I left the house feeling sad and thoughtful. I thought about it, that the terrible truth would dawn on Ruthi slowly but surely. Only on the first day school would she realize that no one was sending any children to her.

Thinking about it made me very sad. I felt that Ruthi, who was so good, didn't deserve this kind of suffering. I decided that if none of the adults were willing to help her, I would have to do it. I didn't know how.

"Hi, Srulik, how's everything?" I heard the happy voice of Asher, my classmate. He had also gone to Ruthi's nursery school.

"Not good," I said, and told him the whole story.

"We have to do something," Asher agreed with me in the end, and both of us kept on walking, deep in thought, until we came to the neighborhood park.

The park was full of little kids. Their parents watched them while sitting on benches all over the park.

"I've got a fantastic idea," I suddenly said. "Let's make a little play."

"A play?" said Asher. "Are you in the mood for it?"

In a few sentences I explained my idea. Asher was enthusiastic. "No problem. Let's start with Danny and Yonatan's mothers."

We practiced the play over and over for a few minutes, and when we knew it by heart, we ran over to the bench where the two mothers who had kids of nursery school age sat. We went really close to the bench. Asher took some marbles out of his pocket and we started to play.

"Do you remember who taught us to play marbles?" I screamed.

"Sure, Ruthi, our nursery school teacher. It

was in this park, remember?" Asher shouted back to me.

From out of the corner of my eye I noticed that the two mothers had stopped talking and were listening to our conversation. That was exactly what we had planned...

"What — you remember Ruthi the nursery school teacher?" I asked and missed the shot.

"Who doesn't remember her?" said Asher. "All my brothers went to her. She's the best nursery school teacher in town."

"All my brothers, too," I boasted. "And I have a lot more brothers..."

"Believe me," said Asher, "I remember her nursery school as if I went there yesterday..."

"And I...," I whispered, "really miss those days." This time I hit two marbles.

The two continued to watch us and most important...to listen.

"I heard that her nursery school is bursting with kids," said Asher, arranging the marbles.

"She told my mother that the ones who get there at the last minute won't be able to get in," I said. (I didn't lie — that's really what Ruthi said.)

"My neighbor signed up her son the minute he was born," said Asher. (He didn't lie, either. It happened six years ago.)

At this point, we started to say things we

hadn't even planned. We remembered together (at the top of our lungs, of course...) how great it was in nursery school, and how we wished we had teachers like that now. From the corner of my eye I saw that the two mothers had started to talk excitedly. I knew we had made the right impression and I hinted to Asher that we should take off.

We left that bench and started to play near another one, where three mothers were sitting.

"Do you remember who taught us to play marbles?" I screamed.

"Who doesn't remember?" shouted Asher.

We went from bench to bench that way. We managed to reach twelve mothers. At one of the benches, the women interrupted our "conversation" and asked about Ruthi's nursery school. They asked questions like, "Does she really care about the children?" "She doesn't just shout over nothing?" "Do you really miss her?"

We praised her to the skies. At a certain point, Asher got overly enthusiastic and started to exaggerate and talk nonsense. I stepped on his foot and shot him a look that only the two of us understood.

"I think the list to sign up is closing soon," I said at the end, just before we left them.

Both of us left the park, and the minute we

were out of sight of the mothers sitting there, we burst out laughing. We enjoyed the play, but more than that, we enjoyed its huge success. "Just wait and see. Tomorrow all the mothers will race over to sign up their kids in Ruthi's nursery school," I said.

And that's what happened. Five women showed up the next day. The day after that, another three. The news went from one to the other, and then they all started to get in a panic, and within three days, there were thirty children signed up for Ruthi's nursery school.

On the fifth day, Ruthi again appeared at our house. Again, she talked with my mother, and suddenly said to her, "Look what a strange thing happened. All of a sudden everyone re-membered to sign up at the same time, just like I told you. I've already signed up thirty children, and there's tremendous pressure on me to accept more. I don't know what to do. Maybe I should take on another teacher..."

When the conversation ended, I found my mother sitting there in complete surprise. "I'm so very happy," she said to me. "You can't imagine how happy I am that the mothers at last decided to act sensibly. It's a good thing I didn't tell her what they were all planning on doing... What's so funny, Srulik? Really..."

I couldn't hold it in and I burst out laughing.

My mother tried as hard as she could to get out of me what was making me laugh, and in the end, I decided to tell her. I told her about the private play Asher and I had put on, and about it's impressive success. When I finished telling her, my mother cried.

"Why are you crying, Imma?" I asked.

"I can't believe that I have such a smart son with such a good heart," my mother said with difficulty. "How did I come to have a son with such a heart of pure gold, how?"

"Did you forget that you sent me to Ruthi's nursery school?" I said.

Two Hundred
Little Plumbers

My name is Yaakov. I live in Jerusalem and
I'm in the fifth grade.

I'm an ordinary boy. I don't stand out in
anything. I'm a little shy, and that makes me
keep quiet even when I should talk.

The school I go to is made up of a few trailers put together. The principal is trying to raise
money to buy a building, but in the meantime,
we're jammed into the old trailers which leak
in the winter and are scorching hot in the
summer.

We don't have a regular playground. Our
playground is a yard full of sand and rocks,
and we have to run carefully so that we don't
fall into a pit or trip over a rock.

On top of all these troubles, a new building
is being built on the next lot, and the people

living there don't especially like us. They would rather we studied in a different place and not run around in front of their eyes and ears, even though they came to live there after we did.

We have a lot of problems with them. Almost every day one of the neighbors shouts at us and at the principal. Sometimes, their complaints make sense — usually not. Like the principal always says to them, "What do you want — for us to chain them to their chairs? Children run around and make some noise. It's not during rest hours, so what do you want from them?"

But the neighbors aren't interested. It seems to me that they were seriously considering the principal's idea of chaining us. Maybe that was just a suspicion on my part. Anyway, what is certain is that they would like us to go away from there as soon as possible.

A week and a half ago, a bulldozer came to the yard of the building next door. It happened that it hit an underground sewage pipe, and a stream of sewage water burst straight into our yard.

Now we really couldn't play because there were a few streams of sewage water running through the yard and we were afraid to fall into them. The smell was unbearable. Worst of all was that the teachers said that it was a health hazard and that we could get sick from it. That really scared us.

A day or two passed. The principal asked the building's residents to fix the leak. But they told him, "Fix it yourself or move your school."

Those were the exact words they used to talk to our principal, who is such an important educator. I wanted to tell them that they should be ashamed of themselves, I wanted to tell them who they were insulting, but I was embarrassed and kept quiet. Deep inside, though, I thought, "What kind of children will they have if that's the bad example they set for them?"

Another two days passed.

We had no choice but to go out and play between the streams of sewage water. Kids in the lower grades even started to play in the water. They didn't understand how dangerous it was, until the principal warned them. Every recess, the teachers talked about the chutzpah of the thing. One of them even suggested calling the police. (How do I know? Because. You probably know how...)

Anyway, the sewage kept on flowing, we suffered, and the principal pleaded with the residents to fix it — but they just laughed in his face.

A week went by, and then I had an idea.

I'm not considered a leader or anything like that, but I always have ideas. The problem is, I'm always embarrassed to say them. But this time my idea was so brilliant, that I decided to overcome my shyness, and whatever would be, would be.

At the end of the first class, I got up my courage and asked the other kids in the class to stay. After the teacher left for the teachers' room, I stood next to the blackboard and announced, "I have an idea how to fight the sewage."

"How?" they all asked.

"We'll go out to the yard now. Each one of us will take out a bucket, and together we'll build a wall that will block the streams of sewage water. Agreed?" I asked excitedly.

"Sure!!!" they shouted. Before I could even say anything, a few kids raced out of the classroom to grab buckets. I ran too. All I needed was to not find a bucket for myself.

In the yard, the amazing work started. The kids in my class ran around dragging huge buckets, whooping excited war cries. It wasn't long before the rest of the classes caught on to what was happening and got into the act. Within ten minutes you could see two hundred kids running energetically, carrying sand and rocks over to the metal fence that separated our yard from the building's yard. I can't describe to you how it looked. I can only try. The yard looked like...like an ant hill. Little kids and big ones, tall and short, fat and thin, carrying buckets, pots, bags, and even thick boards with sand piled up on them. Those who hadn't managed to get something to carry with, used their hands.

In no time at all a wall out of sand and rocks was built, and when the bell rang, the fence was finished. Not even a drop of water could get through.

Loud clapping was heard from the office trailer. It came from all the teachers who had been watching the whole time and who appreciated the good job we did. We all joined in the clapping and quickly went back to our classrooms, tired, yet full of energy.

At the end of the second lesson, we went out to the yard. The sun had completely dried up the wetness, and we could play the way we wanted to.

The next day, when we arrived at school, we again saw streams of sewage water. It turned out that some unknown person had made big holes in the wall we had built to let the water out. We didn't need to guess who had done it...

We went to work, closed up the holes, and during the first recess started to strengthen the

wall. We thickened it, and reinforced the sand and rocks.

The next day, the anonymous person again tried to outwit us. This time he made a small, barely noticeable hole. We easily closed it up. The building's yard filled with a lot of water. The person must have worn boots to get to the wall.

That same day, all the kids in our school worked at covering the wall with boards. Then we covered the boards with sand. It was hard work, but when two hundred kids do it, it's easy and even fun.

The next day, when we got to school, the yard was absolutely dry. The unknown person had, however, tried to push the wall, but it was stronger than he.

Later, the residents of the building called in a special contractor who came with a tractor, removed the sea that had formed in their yard, and after that, repaired the damage.

That same day, the principal came into our classroom and announced that the time had come to stop our building and plumbing work.

"When it's necessary, there's no choice," he said, and added with a smile, "Now we know how hard you're able to work. Let's use it for studies, too."

He turned around and started to leave. But

suddenly he turned, looked for me among the students, and when he found me said, "Yanki, Yanki," and shook his finger in warning.

I smiled. After all, it was a compliment.

I know my principal.

"Hup-sa"

My name is Emmanuel. I live in the northern part of the country.

I'm an average kid, not too quiet and not too wild. I don't have any special problems.

My father works as a garbage collector. Every day, he gets up at four o'clock in the morning and, along with his friends, rushes through the city's neighborhoods to empty the garbage cans into a huge truck. My father is a big, strong man, and he is also the best father in the world (actually, every kid thinks that way about his father). A few times, I asked him to take me to work with him. He never did. He said that there's no sense in waking me up so early.

One time, the teacher asked every kid in class what his father does. When he came to me, I proudly said, "Garbage collector."

The teacher quickly moved on to the next

boy, and I was very hurt that he didn't continue talking to me and asking me details, like he did with the other children.

One time, a bigger kid asked me, "What does your father work at?" I told him, "He collects garbage." He looked at me for a while and then said with a laugh, "Oh, so your father's a garbage truck?"

"My father isn't a truck," I explained to him. "My father works *on* the garbage truck. What's so funny about that?"

Little by little, I started to realize that my father's work was something to be ashamed of. Still, I never for a minute thought of hiding it. Until...

One day, before the teacher came into the classroom, Menashe burst into the room all excited, ran over to me and yelled, "Hup-*sa.*"

I looked at him in shock.

"Hup-*sa*," he repeated and laughed.

When he saw that the other kids didn't understand what he was getting at, he offered to explain. "This morning I saw Emmanuel's father. You won't believe this, but he works on the garbage collection truck. I saw him lift up a huge garbage can, make a 'hup,' dump it into the truck, and then shout to the driver, 'sa.'" (In case you don't know, "*sa*" means "go" in Hebrew.) "Hup-*sa*, Hup-*sa*," chanted Menashe.

The kids started to laugh and I felt like a thousand sharp daggers had been stabbed into my heart. It hurt me a lot. It really hurt me.

I took my bookbag and walked mournfully home from school. I heard the kids shouting behind my back, each one in turn, "Hup-*sa*, Hup-*sa*." I got home. My mother asked me why I had come home early. I answered that I didn't feel well. That was the truth. I didn't tell her why.

When my father came home from work, I burst out crying. Abba showered fast and changed into regular clothes. After that, he came over to me and asked, "What happened, Emmanuel? Why are you crying?"

"Why don't you want me to be a garbage collector?" I asked him.

Abba was startled by my question. "Because I expect you to achieve more than that. Garbage collection is work only for someone who doesn't have any choice. I don't have any choice. I had no other possibility of supporting the family. It is not distinguished work," said my father.

"What *is* distinguished work?" I asked my father.

"For instance...for instance, mayor of the city. That's distinguished work."

"But once I heard them shouting against

him over a loudspeaker, and my friends collected papers on which bad things were written about him. Is that distinguished?" I asked.

Abba sat without saying a word. He sat there in silence for a long time. "You are a smart boy," he said. "I don't have any answer for you. Maybe you are really right."

I told my father the reason I had come home early from school. I saw how he turned pale. His eyes narrowed. He was angry. Oh, how angry he was.

"Pay attention, Emmanuel," he said at last. "It is written: 'Skin a dead animal in the marketplace rather than take charity.' Even the profession most looked down upon is more honorable than taking charity. Don't be ashamed of your father."

The last sentence he said pleadingly. Just imagine that my father had to beg me not to be ashamed of him! It was sad.

The next day when I went to school the taunting didn't stop. It even got worse. I stopped going out during recess because they would run after me yelling, "Hup-*sa*, Hup-*sa*," and tell everyone why.

Those were very hard days, very sad ones, too. I can't even describe to you how sad they were. I don't like to remember those days.

Sometimes kids can be cruel.

On one of those days, when I was walking home from school, a huge garbage truck pulled up beside me. Someone called out to me from the window, "Hey, Emmanuel, how are you?"

I searched in all directions to make sure that no one was watching before I looked up and saw Dubik.

Dubik was my father's best friend, and mine too, if you want to know. Dubik was already a grandfather, and he no longer dragged the heavy garbage cans but drove the truck instead. Once when I was in his house he told me apologetically, "Don't look down at me because I'm only a driver. For twenty-five years I was hanging on the back, and only when I got old did I agree to be a driver."

"Nu, are you getting in?" Dubik shouted, and I rushed to climb up, so that he wouldn't embarrass me.

"Go, go fast," I whispered to him. "They might still see me."

"And if they see you, so what?" wondered Dubik.

"Uh, they...they'll make fun of me even more," I said.

"Who'll make fun of you?" asked Dubik. "Who?"

I told him everything. I told him they had

stopped calling me Emmanuel and started to call me "Hup-sa" instead. I cried as I said it.

The truck stopped next to my house, and Dubik muttered under his breath, "This has got to stop, I won't let it continue." After that he clapped me on the shoulder and said, "Don't worry. I'll take care of it. There's no way they are going to tease a kid because of his father's work." He dropped me off and drove away.

A week passed from the time of our talk when all of a sudden the newspapers started to write that the garbage collectors were planning a strike and that they wouldn't be taking the garbage away. The whole city was afraid of the expected strike because it would be very unpleasant and even dangerous to our health.

A week before the strike was due to start, demonstrations started. Residents demonstrated against the mayor, who wasn't willing to talk with the garbage collectors and hear why they wanted to strike. After strong pressure was put on him, the mayor gave in and notified the workers that he was willing to listen to their demands.

The meeting between the striking workers and the mayor took place in our house.

Two hours before the meeting, my father's friends from work arrived and whispered amongst themselves. I didn't hear what they said. At eight o'clock exactly, the mayor came.

He sat at the head of the table. Dubik sat on one side and my father sat on the other, while the rest of the workers sat or stood around.

"Is your salary too small?" asked the mayor.

"It's enough for us," said Dubik.

The mayor was shocked. "Then why do you want to strike?"

"Because of our children," said Dubik.

"Your children?" the mayor was amazed.

"Yes," said Dubik. "Call Emmanuel."

I ran away from the door so that they wouldn't know I had been listening.

Then the door opened and one of the workers called me in.

"What's your name," asked Dubik.

"Emmanuel," I said, thinking: *As if he doesn't know!*

"And what do they call you in school?" asked Dubik softly.

"Hup-*sa*," I whispered.

"I didn't hear you," said the mayor.

I repeated it.

"Speak up, I can't hear."

"Hup-*sa* is what they call me. Hup-*sa*," I shouted and burst out crying.

My father held me close. Silence filled the room.

"What is the meaning of this?" asked the

mayor, immediately adding, "Actually, I think I understand."

"This boy is not the only one," said Dubik. "My children have all suffered from their friends. My daughter was never once invited to any of the birthday parties the girls in her class made in their homes. My second daughter tried to hide it, but when they found out, they stayed away from her, as if..."

Here his voice broke. "As if my daughter was made of garbage."

At this point all the workers started talking and telling about the suffering their children went through. When I heard some of the stories, I realized that my case was a lot easier than theirs. It turned out that there were some parents who don't let their children be friends with the child of a garbage collector.

The workers talked for a long time. Each one had a chance to say everything that was in his heart. Finally, silence filled the room. We all waited for the mayor's reaction.

For a long time the mayor sat there holding his head in his hands. Then he stood up and declared, "This time you are absolutely right. Let's think of how we can destroy this shameful behavior at its root."

My father sent me out of the room and I went to sleep with my tears still wet. I fell asleep while in the background thunderous voices were heard from the dining room.

The next day I got up as usual. My father had already left the house. I went to school with a heavy feeling. I was afraid that there was no way to solve the problem.

When we went outside for the first break, we saw two garbage trucks parked next to the school building. A few kids started shouting "Hup-sa." All of a sudden, another two trucks appeared, then another three, and then another five. They parked on the sidewalk all along the length of the street. All the kids in school stood on the fence to watch.

We started to count. Ten, twenty, thirty trucks. All the residents of the street left their houses. When the fiftieth truck arrived, the street was closed to traffic. Drivers honked loudly trying to get through the traffic jam. Police patrol cars drove up and the policemen directed all traffic to go down a different street.

Dozens of photographers arrived at the scene, and they took pictures of the garbage trucks from all angles. Everyone knew that something special was about to happen.

About fifty drivers and another hundred workers got off the trucks and waited. Everyone watched to see who they were waiting for. Within a few minutes, a black limousine drove up and from it, the mayor emerged.

He went over to the workers and said, "Are we going?"

They went. To where? To our school. They went in and headed straight for the playground.

All the students surrounded them. It's hard to describe the excitement. No one understood what was going on. On the other side of the fence hundreds of people peered in to see what was happening.

Suddenly, the janitor appeared with the school's large loudspeaker. The photographers aimed their cameras, the reporters took out their notepads, and the mayor began to speak:

"I want to announce that I agree with the demands of the sanitation workers," began the mayor. "They work at the hardest work, and some of the residents of the city act towards them with a lack of gratitude, disparagement, and worst of all, cruelty toward their children."

Now the mayor started to tell the stories he had heard in my house. He told story after story and everyone who heard was appalled. There were stories about kids who had been chased, humiliated, and even hit, when their only crime was that their parents worked at something that wasn't considered distinguished.

"In this school, children tormented a good,

studious boy. 'Hup-sa,' they called him. Where were the rest of the children? Why didn't they go to his rescue?" boomed the principal's voice.

"From now on, if anyone teases one of the sanitation workers' children because of his father's work, the sanitation workers will be allowed to leave that family's garbage next to his front door. Only then will those children be stopped from tormenting their friends for something they didn't do."

With that, the mayor finished his speech and left the school grounds. All the workers did likewise. They climbed into the trucks and started to collect the garbage all over the city. The expected strike was canceled, and I became practically the "hero of the school." In any case, there are not too many kids who have such a big strike called because of them.

Actually, a lot of kids like me benefited from that strike because the story made front-page headlines in all the papers in the country, and within a few days, papers all over the world carried the story. My father showed me a newspaper in French. I didn't understand what was written, but I recognized the photos of the garbage trucks and the mayor speaking, surrounded by children. The mayor received letters of thanks from all over the world in which the garbage workers said that they had the same problem, and that they had decided to adopt the mayor's warning about whoever teases their kids.

Now I'm happy. What I think is really nice is that so many children in the world were saved from shame and humiliation of their friends and all that is a little bit...to my credit.

Behind the Scenes

My name is Na'ama. I live in Jerusalem and the story I want to tell is one that has nothing to do with me, but with someone close to me.

Before I start the story, I want to write something about stories. After that you'll understand the connection.

When a story gets published, most kids look at the cover, breathe in the smell of fresh print and whisper, "What a great book! The stories are so interesting, the artist drew so beautifully!" But I think about the people behind the scenes too — the publisher, the printer, and the editor. If you ask me why — well, it's not just a coincidence that I think about them. My mother is a proofreader. She's the one who fixes the spelling mistakes that creep in during the writing or word processing, and in children's books, she's the one who catches it when a word is used that's too hard.

My sisters and I watch her work and share in her happiness when one of the books she's worked on is published. Whenever I'm in a book store and see children flipping through the pages of books with pleasure, I feel that my mother has a part in it. She proofreads so that the books will be easy to read. Maybe there are kids who don't understand why that's really important. Imagine what would happen if you would read a book with a lot of mistakes, extra letters that got mixed up in the middle of words, and sometimes even terrible, confusing mistakes. My mother says that even after several proofreadings you can still find a lot of mistakes in books, but a book without proofreading has at least ten mistakes on every page. Does that seem exaggerated to you? Ask writers and people who do word processing. They'll tell you.

In most cases, when at long last the book is published, we get a copy from the author (although there were times when they just forgot my mother). Lots of times we wonder why they don't write my mother's name in the book — the work is so hard! Is it hard to write the name of the person who proofread? Don't they deserve it?

Sometimes my mother translates whole books from Hebrew to English. Translation is really like writing, because my mother has to find the right words all over again in the other language. It's a lot harder than checking for spelling and punctuation mistakes, and once it happened that they didn't put her name in, or wrote in small letters "assisted the editor." We saw that it hurt her feelings. But she never said a thing. My mother never complains.

My mother sits for hours and looks in every possible source (dictionary, grammar books), even though she knows all the rules by heart. Sometimes she asks us to help. She asks for our opinion and listens with a smile to our "good" advice.

I hope that the next time a book is published, you will make sure to remember all the dedicated people who work behind the scenes.

They also have a heart. They're also happy when their work is appreciated and sad when they're ignored.

Will you remember my mother?

A Small Money Matter

My name is Aharon. I'm an average kid and very friendly. I like everyone and I love to play and have fun. My father is a rabbi. He has a *kollel*, where married yeshivah students study. He's the head of the *kollel*.

In my story there are a lot of numbers, so whoever doesn't like numbers can go on to the next story.

Every year I have the biggest collection in my class of gogos. That's what we call the apricot pits we play with. I get them several ways. First of all, we have ten children in our house. Ten children, that's something like 70 apricots a week, and 280 in a month. That's not bad. Admit it.

Besides that, I made three shooting boxes. I put them out during breaks between classes in three different places in school. (I watch one, and my two brothers watch the other two, and they get a "percentage" of the gogos they collect and are thrilled.)

Now I want to tell you a secret: Usually, whoever has the box — makes a profit. From my experience, for every twenty gogos that are thrown, only one gets in, and then you need to pay out at least three gogos. (In the ten-point hole, hardly anyone can get it in. In the hundred-point hole, no one gets it in, except for one sharpshooter who sometimes succeeds).

Every day on average I earn from the three boxes about a hundred gogos. Over a month I collected almost 3000 gogos!!!

I liked earning gogos. I don't know why. Once I read a story where it was written that gogos are to kids what money is to big people.

When I read that, I decided that I must be a little stingy, because I never enjoyed my gogos, only collected more and more. The truth is, that sometimes I would also like to shoot at someone else's box, to try to aim and get in the ten-point hole, but I have no time. You've got to understand — my gogo business takes all the time I have during recess (and once even from class, until the teacher warned me that he would throw them all out the window...). I just don't have time. Businessmen, you know.

Two months ago something sad happened in my family. My grandmother died.

My grandmother lived in the building next to us. I loved her very much and I still miss her. My grandmother was very smart and good. She used to make food for us and help us prepare our homework.

I have a lot of things to say about my grandmother, but it's hard for me. I don't like to be sad.

My father said that Grandma is in heaven. He said that she watches us and sees us all the time. My father said that if we learn for Grandma, her soul goes up to heaven and gets to the Heavenly Throne.

I wanted my grandmother to go up to the Heavenly Throne. I also wanted her to know that I, Areh'le, am helping her rise. I started to learn Mishnayos, but I felt that it wasn't enough. I wanted a lot of Mishnayos to be learned for my grandmother.

And then I had an idea.

I took a piece of paper and crayons out of my drawer and drew a sign:

Anyone who is tested by Areh'le on Mishnayos said for my grandmother will get two gogos for each Mishna he learns by heart.

I hung up the sign on the bulletin board next to the playground. I was hoping that kids would learn Mishnayos for my grandmother, and I didn't mind giving two gogos.

What happened was unbelievable.

The entire school came to be tested by me! They were all standing near the doorway to my classroom. I started to test them, but you could hardly hear anything because of the noise and the pushing and shouting.

Our teacher came and someone explained what was happening. I saw him laugh out loud and then ask for quiet.

"Since everyone wants to be tested, we have to make some kind of order. First the fourth grade, Aharon's class, will be tested, and after that we'll start going in order from first grade to the eighth. Within eight days, everyone will be tested. Is that clear?"

Kids from the other classes left disappointed, but ran to their classrooms to review Mishnayos by heart to earn gogos.

I started to test the kids in my class. The first was tested on two Mishnayos and got 4 gogos. The second was tested on 5 and got 10, and the third was tested on 12, and got 24. It wasn't easy for me to see my shoe box full of gogos emptying, but my word is my word.

At the end of the day I took the list of

Mishnayos they had learned. My class was tested on 334 Mishnayos, which cost me 668 gogos.

Almost seven hundred gogos in one day!

The next day I tested the first grade. In first grade they don't learn Mishnayos, and only 8 children were tested on one Mishna. That only cost me 16 gogos. The next day, I tested the second grade, and they were tested on 200 Mishnayos, and that cost me 400 gogos.

The third grade was tested on 326 Mishnayos (652 gogos). The fourth grade had already been tested, so I went on to the fifth. They had been ready for a few days and had learned a lot of Mishnayos. That day I came home with two empty boxes, and for the first time, I was in debt.

They learned 538 Mishnayos. That cost me 1076 gogos! In my boxes I only had 900 gogos. I was in debt for 176 gogos.

I went home and started to add things up. In the meantime, 1406 Mishnayos had been learned in honor of my grandmother, and that made me very happy. "Grandma is definitely watching me and is happy," I thought, but...

I didn't want to think about the debt, but I had to. I counted all my gogos. It turned out that I had 1328 gogos left, out of which I had to pay 176.

From all the thousands I used to have, I was left with 1152. I felt terrible. I didn't want to think about it, but suddenly I saw that my heart was pounding. Maybe you won't understand, and maybe you will, but it's not easy to lose so many gogos in just a few days.

And besides, I had a problem. The sixth, seventh, and eighth grades still hadn't been tested. How would I pay them, I wondered.

That night I couldn't sleep. I tossed and turned and didn't know what to do. I knew that the kids in the sixth grade would be tested on more Mishnayos than the fifth graders. How would I pay them? I thought about it. It was very dark. I heard a voice from the direction of my father's home office. I got out of bed and saw him sitting next to the desk looking at some long papers full of numbers.

"What are you doing, Abba?" I asked him.

"I'm going over the *kollel*'s accounts. There are a lot of people in the *kollel*, Areh'le, and there's not enough money to pay them, and within two days I need to get certain sums of money and I have no idea how I'll get them. It's not easy being a *Rosh Kollel*," my father said.

"Yes, I noticed," I agreed. "From my own experience."

My father gave me a sharp look.

"It's not easy for me either to manage the payment for learning Mishnayos," I explained to my father. "I promised and I don't know how to get them."

"What exactly are you talking about?" my father questioned.

I told him.

My father smiled. I saw his eyes twinkle, and his tired face come to life. Suddenly he started to laugh. "So, you've become head of a *kollel*," he said to me.

"Not exactly," I corrected. "More of a 'Mishnayos Program' in honor of Grandma's memory. It's not exactly the same."

"But almost," said my father.

"Almost," I agreed.

We both sighed. "What are we going to do?" I asked.

"First of all, believe in Providence," said my father, "and besides that, you have to make sure that you'll have a way to pay and not leave your members without any income."

"In the meantime, I have 1328 gogos," I rushed to explain, "and that's enough for 664 Mishnayos. I have no problem with the sixth grade, only with the seventh and eighth."

"Let them know that you're having difficulties, so that they'll know in advance that their payment will be delayed. Don't test them until you make that clear," my father suggested.

And that's just what I did. The next day, I put up another notice:

To all those who want to be tested:
The supply of gogos is running out fast,
and the payment will probably be delayed.
Thanks, Areh'le.

I was afraid they wouldn't agree to come. But they came. The sixth graders were tested on 700 Mishnayos. I was left with a debt of 72 gogos. That same day I came home very worried. I put down my bookbag and went to my bed. I sat there with my eyes open and thought about what to do.

All of a sudden, in walked my brother Moishe. "Areh'le, why aren't you coming with me to count the gogos?"

"What gogos are you talking about?" I said. "I owe 72 gogos and I don't know from where I'm going to get them."

"In the meantime we've won more gogos, silly," my brother said.

"How?" I asked.

"Me and Yirmi" (our younger brother) "sat with the boxes as usual," said Moishe, "and the minute we shouted that all the gogos we'd win would be used for paying the boys who learn Mishnayos, everyone came to throw into our box."

I jumped up from the bed. "You're the greatest!" I said to Moishe. "Let's go count."

We counted together, as usual, ten by ten, and got to 1580 gogos.

I got excited. "Moishe, you are just — great!" I said and hugged him. He was bewildered and didn't understand why I was so excited.

"You get 158 gogos," I remembered his ten percent.

"Okay," he said, "I'm donating them for the Mishnayos."

I felt like I was about to burst from happiness.

The seventh grade learned 950 Mishnayos. I paid the entire 1580. I was left owing 320 gogos. That day my brother Moishe worked extra hours and brought home — you won't believe it — 1560 gogos. Again, Moishe gave his share for the Mishanayos.

Then it was the last day, the eighth grade's test. I came with a few boxes filled with gogos. Even before class started I paid off my debts (320) and waited for recess. I had 1240 gogos left.

It was a strange sight — the eighth graders being tested by a kid in the fourth grade. Every single one of them was tested on practically a whole *Masechet*. I saw right away that the amount I would need would be huge. That day I managed to test ten kids. The rule was that the gogos were paid out all together at the end of the test. I was happy that I had some breathing space.

Actually, they didn't treat the test that seriously, and were even less serious about the tester, namely me. They viewed the whole thing as fun, but they really did know all the Mishnayos by heart and that's what counts.

Within three days I finished testing everyone. That day I went home, took out a pocket calculator and started to add up the numbers. When I finished, I thought I had made a mistake. I did it again. It was a huge amount. I was happy that they had learned so many Mishnayos, but I knew that I'd never in a million years be able to pay such a large amount. They learned 2800 Mishnayos, and I owed them 5600 gogos.

Together with my brother, I started to count all the gogos we had collected during the past three days.

A thousand, two thousand, three thousand, three thousand five hundred. That was it. How would I get another 2100 gogos?

"Moishe, it looks to me like we don't have

enough. Maybe I should sit next to the box with you tomorrow and help you?"

Moishe didn't answer. Finally he said, "Listen, Areh'le, no one's shooting anymore, the gogo season has ended and they've already started making them '*hefker*.'" (That's when you throw all the gogos you've collected into the playground and whoever wants to can take them.) "The gogos I brought yesterday and the day before, were from *hefker*. You don't know how I fought for every gogo, I really got hurt...and now...there's no way we're going to be able to earn even a hundred gogos, and you're talking about two thousand?" Both of us sat there in silence. How come I didn't notice that the season had ended? Me, the big expert on gogos...

Suddenly I knew why I had become an expert on Mishnayos — it was a lot better. But still, debts have to be paid. So what was I supposed to do?

It was hard for me to sleep that night. In the morning I went to school carrying all the thousands of gogos. During the first break, I headed for the eighth grade. I waited for the class, which went a little bit overtime, to finish.

In a sad voice I said, "I apologize. I have here 3500 gogos, and I owe you 5600. I promise you that I'll do everything I can to get the rest soon.

Hey — why are you laughing?" The kids in the eighth grade were holding their stomachs and laughing hard. I didn't understand why.

Suddenly Avi, a serious, mature boy who looks much older than his age, came over to me. "Look, what's your name? Areh'le? We don't collect gogos. Listen, it's not for our age..."

"Wait a minute — then why did you let yourselves be tested?"

"We let ourselves be tested to honor your grandmother's memory. We really liked the notice you wrote, and we decided to participate in the contest and raise the number of Mishnayos. But gogos? Don't insult us!"

They helped me carry the boxes of gogos to my classroom. There were ten minutes left to recess. I went over to the window and shouted:

"*Hefker!*"

Pyramid

My name is Davidi. I live in Petach Tikvah and I am in the second grade.

We have six kids in our family, four boys and two girls.

We were born about a year and a half apart. My oldest brother is fourteen and a half. He is already studying in a *yeshivah ketanah*.

I think that there is practically no family where the kids get along as well together as in our family. We hardly ever fight. The opposite. Each one thinks about the other and is considerate of him. Each one lets the other play with his toys, and no one bosses anyone else around.

And most important — no one is jealous of the other. My father says that this is the secret of our family. It's built so that no one is jealous.

You're going to ask, "How?" I'll tell you. My father always repeats to me and my brothers and sisters our family rules. He has to do it, because otherwise we wouldn't know how to treat each other.

My father says that problems between brothers and sisters start with jealousy. When a kid thinks that his father loves his brother more or gives his brother more things than he gets, then that kid starts to be angry with his brother, with his father, and with the whole world. And besides, it makes him feel bad and sad.

My father says that it's not right to give children the feeling that they're equal. Because the minute you give one something, then they'll all think, "Why not me?"

That's why, my father explained to us, our family is built like a pyramid: whoever is bigger, is more important. Just like that. The oldest is the most important. There's no one more important than he is. The second one needs to honor the oldest, the third needs to honor the second, and so on. According to this rule, no one can come with complaints like, "Why did you give to my older brother?" The answer is: "Because he's bigger and deserves it." And so that everyone will feel okay about it, each one of us has a younger brother who honors him. For instance, Yossi honors Reuvi (the oldest), but Esti honors him. Nechama honors Esti — and Ushi honors Nechama. I honor Ushi and...

Yup. You get the problem. There's no one to honor me. I asked about it a few times and every told me, "Wait until another child will be born. We also went through a time when we didn't have a little brother or sister and we waited."

Only they waited about a year and a half at the most (except for Nechama who waited two years), but I've been waiting for seven years already and no other child has been born.

I don't make a big deal out of it, because it's not bad for me at all. I'll tell you why. Since all my brothers and sisters (except for me) feel that they're bigger than at least one person, they don't act bad at all. They act very nice because whoever is bigger helps the younger one a lot, especially since the younger one honors him. No one tries to say, "Why do I have to and he doesn't," because each one knows where he stands and knows who's more important than him and who he's more important than.

So it turns out that they all love me and spoil me because I have to honor all of them. Get it?

There's another good part that I forgot to tell you. You won't believe this, but when it comes to punishments, the pyramid is upside-down!

For instance, once all the boys went to the pool and came home late. Reuvi got the biggest punishment, because he is the oldest and he is more important, and that's why my parents expect more from him. Yossi also got punished, but less than Reuvi. Ushi got a small punishment, and I didn't get any. My father said to them, "He can't come back without you. You are to blame that he was late," and skipped over punishing me. Not one of my brothers was mad about it. They all thought it was right and knew that that was the price they had to pay for being bigger and getting respect from the younger ones.

My brothers really deserve all this respect. They care about me so much. Each one cares about the one younger than he is and in exchange, they honor him. Sometimes I'm not sure what's better — to be big and respected and to be responsible for everyone, or to be little and only get...

But anyway, believe me, it bothered me a lot that I was the littlest and that there was no one under me. I didn't tell anyone, but inside I felt that I was really missing something.

Lately our house is being redecorated. They made two rooms bigger, and one of them they turned into a new boys' room, with brand new furniture. Yesterday they came and delivered the chest of drawers and the beds.

We wanted to make the beds but suddenly Abba said, "Wait a minute — no one's going to sleep. First we'll wait for Reuvi to come home from yeshivah."

"What for?" we asked. "We never wait for him."

"True," said Abba, "but now we need to know where you'll sleep and we need to let Reuvi, the oldest, have the honor of choosing which bed he prefers."

We all nodded in agreement. Me too. But inside I felt really sad. I wanted to scream. I felt they weren't being fair to me. I really wanted to sleep on the bed next to the wall, and I knew that I had practically no chance of getting it. I always thought my father's idea about the pyramid was a good one, but this time I was very much against it. Did I always have to be the last one? Did I always have to give in to everyone — to give respect to all my brothers and let them get what they want? My heart twisted in pain, but I didn't say a thing. I escaped to the bathroom and burst out crying. I tried hard to make sure that no one would hear me. I didn't want to ruin my father's pyramid.

After that, I put water on my face so that no one would see I had been crying. I hadn't needed to. No one was looking at me anyway.

They were all looking at the beautiful new children's room. Everyone was waiting for Reuvi to come.

Reuvi arrived and said a nice warm hello as usual. Everyone jumped on him. "Choose a bed! Pick one already!"

"What do you want from me?" Reuvi asked Abba. Abba explained to him that we had all been waiting for two hours for him to come home so that the each one of the four boys could chose, according to age, the bed he wanted.

Reuvi came into the room. I watched him anxiously. I saw that everyone was doing the same. I saw him glance at the bed next to the desk. After that, he looked at the three beds behind it. I prayed that he wouldn't chose the one next to the wall. I closed my eyes tensely and suddenly I heard him say...

"Let Davidi chose first."

I opened my eyes in astonishment. Everyone was surprised. Something like this had never happened before.

"What happened?" asked Abba.

"I thought that it wasn't fair that everyone honors me but *I* don't have a brother to honor. For a long time I've thought about it, that the pyramid idea is a wonderful idea, and that because of it our family is so close and loving.

But, all these years I've also thought that it has two minuses. One, that I have no brother to honor, and two, that there's no one to honor the last child. Now I've decided to solve both problems at the same time. I'll honor Davidi. That way I'll also be able to honor someone, and Davidi will have someone to honor him. Do you agree?"

We all said in unison, "We agree!" I saw on their faces that they were happy for me. Abba hugged Reuvi (who's a little embarrassed when he's hugged), and said, "Who would have believed that not only did my son follow in my path, but even found ways to improve it." Reuvi answered him, "Abba, the fact that I thought of it is only because of this method, which gives each child the honor coming to him. I didn't improve it, Abba. I only followed in your path and just found it."

It was a very emotional scene. We suddenly felt like such a close family. It was just great.

"Davidi, choose already," I heard Ushi say. Suddenly I didn't care at all about which bed to pick. I just promised myself one thing.

"I want to sleep in the bed next to Reuvi," I heard myself say.

Between Me and My Mother

My name is Nechama. I'm twelve and go to Bais Yaakov and am the oldest of six children.

I have two wonderful parents. My father works hard and is practically never home, and my mother is a medical secretary.

I want to tell you a little bit about my relationship with my mother. I love her a lot, but for some reason, I just don't get along with her. Worse, we actually fight all the time.

For instance, when I want to talk with her about a teacher who picked on me or a another one who gives a lot of tests, my mother always takes the side of the teachers. Sometimes she says it as a joke, but I feel very hurt and answer her back, and then we start to get mad (because we both have very sharp tongues).

This problem really bothers me, because my

mother is the one closest to me and knows me better than anyone else. She understands me very well, and when we talk in a relaxed conversation, it's so beautiful and nice. The problem is that sometimes I say things and she teases me or says that the other side is right, and then I get back at her and a big fight starts. Sometimes I'm really fresh to her and then afterwards I apologize, and she doesn't always forgive me, or she answers me back something and I don't hold back, and again...

The atmosphere in the house is not good because of these fights and my mother complains that she is miserable and to be pitied, and I feel like I'm bad. That's why I try not to tell her things, so that it won't start a fight, but it's hard, because I don't have anyone else to tell things to.

I did have one good friend, but our friendship didn't last because she had a different friend, a better one, who didn't let her be friends with me because she thought that I came between their friendship (it didn't really bother me that much). So, as a matter of fact, I don't have a single true, good friend except for my mother, and about that kind of friendship I already told you...

Not long ago I told my father about it. (As a matter of fact, I didn't need to tell him. He can see the situation himself.) At first, he took it calmly, because he's already used to his daughter fighting with her mother all the time. I told him that I don't have any friends, and that Imma is my only friend, and that she... And here I burst into tears and I couldn't stop crying. I felt that I couldn't go on like that any more, without anyone to confide in. When I started to cry, I saw Abba wake up from his indifference. He calmed me down and said in plain and simple terms that I must understand that Imma has to act like a mother. "Because you talk to her like a friend, you think that you can fight with her, just like you fight with your friends. It's not like that. You have to honor your mother. You can't expect the same equality with your mother as you have with your friends. You're sometimes allowed to even sharply criticize a friend. But with a mother, that's being fresh. You're not allowed to be fresh to Imma.

"I understand you," said Abba. "Because you are open with Imma, you sometimes forget that she's not another friend of yours but just so happens to be your mother. But Imma doesn't forget it, and she's not allowed to forget it. She needs to raise and educate you, even if friends aren't usually supposed to do that."

My father had given me food for thought. I

always enjoyed my father's wisdom and his ability to explain what I was feeling. He was right this time too. I expected my mother to act like a friend. And a friend who points out shortcomings is irritating and causes fights. But my mother is not only a friend but a mother.

My father told me that there are two solutions. One is for my mother to stop talking with me as a friend and slowly but surely get used to being "only" a mother. And the second, is for me to take it upon myself to have a special kind of friendship with my mother, one where I will have to honor my friend. I can think differently from her and even tell her so, but I can never be fresh, only respectful. A "one-way friendship," he called it.

It's easy for me to see that the second solution is the best one for me. The question is, will I be able to do it?

Brave or Scaredy Cat

My name is Eliav. I'm ten years old and I go to the Ma'ale Torah school in Ma'ale Adumim. I'm in the fifth grade.

I read KIDS SPEAK and MORE KIDS SPEAK and I also want to tell about myself.

A year ago, on Lag Ba-Omer, all my friends from the youth group I'm a member of made a joint bonfire, just like every year.

For weeks we collected all the pieces of wood and cartons and one day after Ma'ariv we went down into the wadi that's next to our neighborhood and lit the bonfire.

The air was filled with the good smells of roasting potatoes, onions, and marshmallows. We sang and were happy. One of our counselors started to tell us a scary story with a funny ending. We were having a lot of fun. Suddenly, we heard Arab voices from the distance. At first, we didn't pay any attention. We thought it was the sound of the wind. But all of sudden we realized that they were real voices. Three figures wearing keffiya's came out of the wadi. One of them was holding a stick. We started to feel scared. A few kids said, "Who's afraid? We'll finish them off in a minute," but most of the kids, me included, realized that it was serious and we started to run.

As I was running I saw one of the counselors lying on the ground, tied up with cables. I didn't need any more than that. I just ran as fast as I could along with the rest of the kids towards home.

When I got home, only my sister was there. My parents had gone to a wedding. I told her everything. She was afraid and went downstairs to our neighbors to ask them what we should do. I stayed in the house. I was nervous and decided that I should call the police.

I dialed 100 (when I think back, I realize that I should have called the city police station in Ma'ale Adumim, and not Jerusalem). A man's voice answered me: "Police, shalom," and before he could say a word, I started to tell him the story fast. At first he was suspicious, and said, "Listen, kid, it's not a joke, it's the police," and I started to cry. Then the policeman realized that the matter was serious. He transferred me to a different policeman, one probably higher up, and I had to tell him the whole story all over again. In the middle of the conversation I heard him say, "Send out a squad car." Then he told me not to be afraid and that I should stay by the phone and wait for a call. From time to time they called, and every time a different policeman would ask for more details.

Suddenly I heard the sound of a siren coming from the wadi. I couldn't understand how they had gotten there so fast, but my sister, who had come back in the house, said that she had called the local police from the neighbor's phone.

Ten minutes later, the phone rang, and this time it was a policewoman on the line, and she said to me, "Don't worry, everything's okay. It was only your counselors' friends who took a joke too far and were fooling around. We took them in for questioning and if we need any help, we'll call you. Good night," she said and hung up.

The next Shabbos, my friends started to make fun of me, saying, "Scaredy cat, go cry to the police." Since then, they haven't let up. Even now, they tease me. But I know that I did the right thing at the right time. A few other kids and counselors think the same way.

I think that if you feel that there's danger,

you shouldn't be afraid but should call anyone who might be able to help. I know that if it had been real Arabs, everyone would have praised me, and the police would have even called me a hero. What would happen if every kid and adult thought that people were just fooling him and joking, and walked right by?

I think that I acted the right way and I'm telling you, Chaim, that if the same thing were to happen again, I would run again to call the police. What do you think? Am I right?

Inner Journey

My name is Yechiel. I'm in the fourth grade.

I'm skinny and weak. In school work, I'm average — not good and not bad. And I have one serious problem.

I have no friends.

The kids in my class aren't friends with me, and even worse, a lot of them pick on me and make trouble for me.

I don't know what they want from me. Maybe it's because I'm not strong, or maybe it's because they just can't stand me. I guess I can understand them. There's nothing special about me that would make anyone want to be my friend, so why should they want to?

Every recess I have some kind of "run-in" with one boy or another. It's really the opposite, that they have a run-in with me. They just come and start picking on me. Sometimes they only hurt my feelings and sometimes they push, and even hit. They don't explain why they do it. I guess it's because they don't have any explanation. After all, I don't do anything to them.

Until yesterday I would go home every day feeling very bad. I felt that I didn't have anything to do in school. If it were you, you'd feel the same way.

But after what happened yesterday, I think there's a chance that everything will change.

Yesterday our school had a class trip. Everyone's been talking about it for the past week. Not with me.

I didn't even know where we were going. They gave me a note, and my mother signed it and put it in an envelope with some money, and I gave it to the teacher. I knew that on Wednesday I wasn't supposed to come with a bookbag, but with a backpack instead. Aside from that, I didn't know a thing. I only asked myself if on a day like this they would bother me more or less. On the one hand, there were no classes, and the kids would have more time to start up with me. But on the other hand, I thought, maybe they would be so busy enjoying the trip they would forget about me.

You can be sure I wasn't too excited about this trip. If it had been up to me, I would have stayed home. Not just on the day of the trip, but every day. But kids have to go to school, and not stay home. That's why I go.

On the day of the trip I got up a little late. I rushed to school and thought that maybe I would miss the bus. I wasn't late. It was standing there and I went in through the back door and sat down next to a window.

The bus pulled away and I looked at the road, the cars, the houses quickly passing us by, and then I noticed that the scenery was changing, and on all sides there was only road and fields.

Then I heard a voice. "What are you doing here, Sonny?" It was Rabbi Greenwald, the eighth grade teacher.

"I-I'm sitting," I said to him.

"I noticed," said Rabbi Greenwald. "But why here?"

"Is this the rabbi's seat?" I asked. "I'll move to a different place."

I heard a few kids laughing. I looked in their direction and suddenly saw that I didn't know them.

"What grade are you in?" asked Rabbi Greenwald.

"Fourth," I said. "I don't see a single kid from my class here."

Everyone burst out laughing. They weren't laughing at me, but at what I said. I had never been able to make kids laugh.

Rabbi Greenwald looked at me in amusement. I saw that he wasn't angry. "Do you mean to tell me that you didn't notice that you didn't get on the right bus?"

"It's not a matter of right or not right," I answered to the sound of the eighth graders' laughter. "It's a matter of there was only one bus and I got on."

Even Rabbi Greenwald burst out laughing. I saw that he was enjoying our talk.

"Wait a minute, just wait a minute," he laughed. "Do you mean to tell me that you didn't look around to find your friends from your class?"

"I don't have any friends in my class," I answered. "I don't have any friends."

The smile still stayed on the faces of the teacher and students, but the laughter suddenly stopped. Then the smiles disappeared after it.

"What does that mean, that you don't have any friends?"

"That means that I don't care who I go with, because the only friend I have is the bus window."

I was surprised at myself, how I found the words to talk like that. I mean, at home I always knew how to talk and had a "big mouth," but in school I was always quiet.

"So you don't care if you go with us?" asked Rabbi Greenwald.

"No," I said. "What difference does it make to me?"

He was shocked by what I said. After a few minutes he said, "But we have a problem. Your class' trip ends at two, and ours at nine-thirty at night. What should we do?"

I thought a little. "I don't know, but don't worry — I won't get off in the middle."

The laughter began again. Everyone sitting in the bus from the two eighth grade classes just stood up, looked at me and laughed at every word I said. The whole thing was entertaining for them. I guess my answers were, too.

"But your parents will be waiting for you at two," I heard the teacher say. "We have to notify them."

And that's what happened. The driver phoned in a message to his office in Bnei Brak and within five minutes they let him know that they had called my parents who had given permission for me to return at nine-thirty.

I went back to looking at the scenery outside the window. All of a sudden, a boy from the eighth grade sat down next to me. I didn't know his name. He looked like he was already in yeshivah. Big like that.

He stated to talk with me, asking me about

my class. I told him the plain truth about my situation in class, and why it wasn't at all good for me there.

He was very surprised. "Do you know something? A kid like you, so smart and entertaining, should be the star."

"Star?" I said. "What's that?"

"That's a kid who's so friendly and great that everyone likes him," he said.

"If so, then I'm a falling star," I said.

"How do you know what a falling star is?"

"I read," I said briefly. "Books are the only friends I have."

The boy and some of his friends looked at me in surprise. They didn't know what to say.

"I think that you should stop feeling sorry for yourself," said the boy, whose name I already knew was Baruch. That's what his friends called him.

I didn't know what he meant.

"If you have a problem, you have to try to solve it and not be busy all the time feeling sorry for yourself. You have a lot of possibilities of succeeding and getting in with the gang."

"Not true," I said, "I'm so skinny and weak."

"Why do you have to be fat and strong?" asked Baruch. "What are you — a class of dock workers?"

He had managed to make me laugh. I was

rolling with laughter. He got encouraged by my laugher and kept on talking. "You're a smart kid. You have a mouth, I would even say a big mouth. The minute you show the others just a little of what you know and stop feeling sorry for yourself all the time, you'll see that they'll treat you with more respect."

I shrugged my shoulders.

We got to the first stop of the trip. First we ate breakfast in the "Woods of the Forty," next to Mt. Carmel in Haifa, and after that we started off on a very hard hike.

It was a steep path going down and you needed to be very careful walking so that you wouldn't slip and fall. The teacher held on to me on one side, and Baruch on the other. I told them that I didn't need it. A few times I even wriggled free of them and went by myself. I enjoyed every minute.

After two hours, we finished the hike and went by bus to a place called "Hoshaya View." Over there we rode on donkeys. It was the greatest.

After we finished riding, I discovered that my food was all finished. I didn't say any thing, but one of the students, Shimon was his name, told me, "Let me see your backpack." I gave it to him and he saw that it was empty.

"Okay guys, let's all chip in with some food," Shimon shouted to everyone.

In a minute, my backpack was full of snacks, cookies, drinks, and I even got two rolls. "Stop — I could travel to Europe with this," I said.

We ended the trip with a super boat ride on the Kinneret and after that we started the ride home towards Bnei Brak.

On the way back, I talked with Baruch for a long time. I don't remember the conversation exactly, but it gave me more self-confidence. He told me that if I feel that I'm a successful kid — I'll succeed. And if I think that I'm a kid to be pitied and not successful, I'll fail.

In the middle of his talking, I fell asleep. I must have slept the whole way. Anyhow, that trip wasn't really for a kid my age.

A hand woke me up. "We're back in Bnei Brak," Baruch whispered to me. "Wake up."

I woke up. I looked out the window and saw the streets so familiar to me. In my heart I felt very happy, like I had never felt before. The bus drove closer to my street. On the way, it stopped at a bus stop and some of the boys got off.

When we got to my house, Baruch said, "I'll walk you to the entrance."

He got off with me and when we got there,

he said to me, "And besides that, I want you to know that from today on you have a lot of friends. Not only me. The whole eighth grade is friends with you starting from today. I want you to know that we really enjoyed being with you. You are just one great kid." He clapped me on the shoulder and ran back to the bus.

I slept like a log. I never felt as good. I knew there was a chance that everything would change.

Today, I went back to my class. My classmates, who didn't know what happened to me, started to tease me. "Where did you take your trip? In the classroom? Did you miss the bus?"

But, unlike the times before, I didn't keep quiet. "I went on the eighth grade trip," I said and started to describe to them everything we did on the trip. I wasn't afraid of them and their reactions any more. I remembered very well what Baruch had said.

When I first started talking, they still wanted to bother me, but during the rest of my story all the kids in my class stood around me and listened.

When the bell rang at the end of recess, right before the teacher came in, Baruch came to the class. He looked and saw me talking, surrounded by kids, and he smiled. "Come visit us in the eighth grade," he announced. "What?

That's how you leave good friends?"

I smiled. I knew he wanted to help me.

But it looked to me like he wouldn't need to help me anymore. His talk with me on the trip had already helped me enough. I'm not going to sink in self-pity again. Instead I want to make sure, *b'ezras Hashem*, to get myself out of the situation I find myself in.

Because besides the trip that I enjoyed, there was another journey — an inner journey.

Glossary

The following glossary provides a partial explanation of some of the Hebrew, Yiddish, and Aramaic words and phrases used in this book. The spellings and explanations reflect the way the specific word is used herein. Often, there are alternate spellings and meanings for the words.

ABBA: Daddy

ACHARONIM: major Halachic authorities after the mid-16th century

AMORA: a Sage immediately following the Mishnaic period

AVINU, AV HARACHAMAN: Our Father, merciful Father

AVREICH CHASHUV: important married yeshivah student

B'EZRAS HASHEM: with G-d's help

BAIS YAAKOV: a network of girls' schools

BENTCHER(S): pamphlet(s) of blessings

BIRCAS HAMAZON: Grace after meals

BLI AYIN HARA: may there be no Evil Eye!

CHEDER: Talmud Torah, school for young boys

DAVEN: (Y.) to pray

ERETZ YISRAEL: the Land of Israel

HAMOTZI: blessing said before eating bread

HASHEM: G-d

HATZALA: volunteer emergency ambulance service

HEFKER: ownerless

IMMA: Mommy

KIDDUSH LEVANA: blessing the moon

KIPPA: yarmulke

KOLLEL: Torah study center for married students

MA'ARIV: evening prayers

MASECHET: tractate of the Talmud

MEZONOS: cooked grain products

MIDDOS: character traits

MINCHA: afternoon prayers

MOTZAI SHABBOS: after the Sabbath

PEYOS: side curls

RASHI: commentator on the Mishna

RISHONIM: great Halachic authorities and commentators of the
    11th to 16th centuries

ROSH CHODESH: the beginning of the Jewish month

ROSH KOLLEL: dean of a Kollel

SHABBOS: the Sabbath

SIDDUR: a prayer book

SUGYA: Talmudic topic

TA'AMEI HAMIKRA: the melody markings for Torah readings

TANNA: Sage of the Mishnaic period

TATTE: Daddy

TEHILLIM: Psalms

TOSAFOS: early commentary on the Talmud

TOVIM ME'OROT: "Good are the Luminaries"

YESHIVAH KETANAH: Torah school for thirteen- to sixteen-year-old
    boys

Kids SPEAK

Children Talk about Themselves

by Chaim Walder

This very special book created a new genre in children's books: a book in which children themselves speak out about their problems, fears, joys, and unusual experiences. An overwhelming success with young readers — and with their parents and teachers too — *Kids Speak* has been translated into several languages. And words from the heart — as expressed by Yoni, Meir, Rafi, Chava, Rivky, Malki, and twenty-eight other children — are understood by all.